"In thirty years recruiting leaders across industries and reading countless leadership books, I've rarely encountered a perspective as distinctive as Lifrieri's. His ability to blend intelligence with emotional awareness allowed him to navigate the chaotic, high-stakes world of law enforcement with rare effectiveness. Readers will find his insights both compelling and genuinely unique."

—Jeff Wierichs, Senior Partner, Global Executive Search, Korn Ferry International

"Lifrieri captures the essence of leadership forged in crisis. After four decades in risk management, I've seen leaders who inspire and leaders who make you question every decision. This is someone I'd want in the trench during the worst of times."

—Antony Ainsworth, Chief Commercial Officer, Global Insurance Risk Management

"From his decorated professional experience and well-seasoned judgment, Detective Lifrieri guides us to safety by explaining how the world is; rather than how we wish it to be. He has clearly seen and remembered all for the reader's benefit."

—Honorable Mario M. Kranjac

LEADING
THROUGH
CHAOS

LEADING THROUGH CHAOS

WHAT DECADES IN INTELLIGENCE, CRISIS,
AND CHAOS TAUGHT ME ABOUT LEADERSHIP

SAL LIFRIERI

Dedication

To Chief Donald Moss

You taught me the best leadership lesson I ever received, though I never got the chance to tell you. When I thought I was burned out, you gave me a chance to shine. You didn't just open a door; you showed me I still had something worth walking through it for. The career I built, the leader I became, all trace back to that moment, and to you. I am who I am today because you saw something in me I couldn't see in myself.

To Jim Henry

For over twenty years, you were the rock behind me. Steady, certain, always there to learn from. You never realized the effect you had on people, especially me. The success I've found in this second phase of my career exists because of what you taught me, not through grand gestures, but through quiet consistency and unshakable integrity. You are missed daily, and you always will be.

Great leaders don't just change the trajectory of a career.

They change the person holding it. You both did that for me.

This book is for both of you.

CONTENTS

ACKNOWLEDGEMENTS

Some books are written alone. This one wasn't.

To Annmarie Sabath, my "Book Sister," — you removed the fear I didn't realize I was carrying. When the blank pae felt impossible, you made it approachable. When the doubt crept in, you provided the roadmap. This book exists because you believed it should, and you showed me how.

To Carla Blum — you've been there through every version of this journey, when no one else knew what I was building. Your encouragement didn't just lift me up in the tough times; it reminded me why the work mattered. Thank you for never letting me quit.

To Michael Micciche Jr. — your research, your attention to detail, and your behind-the-scenes work were as essential to this book as the words themselves. You didn't just assist; you built the scaffolding that held everything together. This wouldn't be what it is without you.

To Michael Micciche Sr. — twenty years of scattered thoughts and handwritten notes don't become a book on their own. You took the chaos and gave it structure. More than that, you've been both a trusted advisor and a good friend, knowing when to push and when to listen. You helped me see the finish line when I couldn't.

To Judy Raboin — you kept the daily chaos at bay so I could focus on the work that mattered. You didn't just manage my calendar; you managed the distractions, the interruptions, the noise that pulls focus from what actually needs doing. You handle my day-to-day life so I don't have to, and I would be lost—literally lost—without you. This book exists because you made sure I had the time and space to write it.

To Christine McQuillan — spunky, tenacious, hard-driven, and relentless in the best possible way. You never slowed down, never settled for good enough, and never let me settle either. You were always ready to help with the creative, always willing to challenge an idea that wasn't working, always making me stop and think. What you can create is amazing.

Writing about chaos is one thing. Surviving it long enough to finish the book is another. I didn't do that alone, and I'm grateful I didn't have to.

Thank you.

SAL LIFRIERI

ABOUT THE AUTHOR

Sal Lifrieri is a recognized security and counterterrorism expert with over 40 years of experience navigating crises, conducting threat assessments, and leading under pressure. As President and founder of Protective Countermeasures Inc. (PCC Secure), he provides consulting, training, and investigative services to Fortune 100 companies across diverse industries, including commercial real estate, energy, global entertainment, financial institutions, and legal firms.

Sal spent 20 years with the New York Police Department, achieving the prestigious rank of Detective First Grade. He served as a member of the elite NYPD Hostage Negotiation Team, certified as both a negotiator and emergency psychological technician. His assignments included creating the NYPD's Russian Organized Crime Project, conducting major case investigations at local and federal levels, and directing the Protective Operations Unit within the Intelligence Division, where he oversaw protective intelligence and threat investigations for the Mayor of New York and key elected officials.

As Director of Security and Intelligence Operations for New York City's Office of Emergency Management, Sal's work included crisis and contingency planning for the city and its corporate residents, as well as coordinating with intelligence and anti-terrorism operations with city, state, federal, and international agencies. He oversaw the security design and buildout of New York City's Emergency Operations Center during the critical pre-9/11 era.

A frequent media commentator on terrorism and security, Sal often appears on networks including ABC, CNN, Fox News, NBC, and international networks such as the CBC. He has lectured at the U.S. Department of Defense Marshall Center for International Security Studies in Germany on crisis and consequence management and served as a Certified Technical Assistance Provider for the U.S. Department of Justice, conducting threat and vulnerability assessments for state and local jurisdictions. He has taught courses on terrorism, crisis management, executive protection, and stalking at Iona University and Fordham University.

Sal served as past President of the Empire Chapter of IALEIA (International Association of Law Enforcement Intelligence Analysts), the world's largest professional organization representing law enforcement analysts. His board positions include former Executive Vice President and board member at Diversified Security Services (AMEX: DVS) and current membership on Securitas's Client Advisory Board. Other non-profit boards include Lincoln Hall Boys Haven in Somers, NY, Achilles International, and the Union League Club.

Leading Through Chaos distills decades of frontline experience into a leadership manual for navigating uncertainty, making it his most personal and practical work to date.

INTRODUCTION

Leadership books love to celebrate success. They parade case studies of visionary CEOs, military generals who never lost a battle, and crisis managers who made all the right calls at the right moments. They're filled with inspiring quotes, tidy frameworks, and reassuring messages that leadership is something you master through positive thinking and a solid action plan.

This isn't that book.

This is a book about failure: leadership, systems, and spectacular human failure. It's about the moments when everything that could go wrong did, often because someone in charge couldn't get out of their own way. It's about ego, politics, bureaucratic dysfunction, and the uncomfortable truth that we're often safe not because of our systems but in spite of them.

And it's about what happens when you finally learn to recognize the patterns that predict disaster before it arrives.

The "why" is what this book is about, not just what went wrong, but the deeper patterns of human behavior and organizational dysfunction that make the same mistakes inevitable unless someone has the awareness and discipline to stop them.

The stories you're about to read are real. The failures are real. Many involve people in positions of enormous responsibility who make choices ranging from merely incompetent to genuinely dangerous. I've changed names and identifying details where necessary, but the essence of each story, including human behavior, the organizational dysfunction, and the moment when someone should have known better, is exactly as it happened.

You'll read about the mother who accidentally roasted her infant and the toddler I found on the bedroom floor, asking for juice. About the murder of nine-year-old Shemika Jennings and the conversation with a police chief that changed my career. About walking into the NYPD Intelligence Division and finding that the people who knew everything didn't know I was coming. About the business of fear that emerged after 9/11, when "credible threats" became currency and overreaction became policy. About a TSA agent who confiscated cuticle scissors from a pilot seated next to an ax. About a Navy officer who couldn't provide security for a pier because of jurisdictional protocols, even though her ship was tied to that same pier.

These aren't just war stories. They're case studies of what happens when systems prioritize compliance over comprehension, when leaders mistake activity for progress, and when organizations value the appearance of control over actual safety.

This book is organized chronologically through my career, but it's not a traditional memoir. Each chapter uses real events to illustrate specific leadership principles, or, more accurately, to show what happens when those principles are ignored. You'll see how poor communication between agencies can undermine even the most critical operations. How the ego can transform competent professionals into obstacles. How political considerations can override common sense. How fear can paralyze decision-making or, worse, drive organizations toward performative actions that create the illusion of safety without reality.

The tone is candid because sugarcoating failure teaches no one anything. It's gritty because these are stories from crime scenes and command centers, not boardrooms or TED talks. It's often darkly humorous because sometimes the only response to breathtaking incompetence is laughter, or you'd go insane. And it's unflinchingly honest about human behavior.

If you're expecting a book that will make you feel good about leadership, this isn't it. If you want a simple checklist that promises to solve all your problems, look elsewhere. But if you're willing to confront uncomfortable truths about how decisions actually get made under pressure, and if you want practical tools for recognizing when you're about to make the same mistakes that have derailed countless leaders before you, then keep reading.

Because chaos doesn't destroy leaders. It reveals them. The question isn't whether you'll face pressure, dysfunction, or crisis. You will. The question is whether you'll have the awareness to recognize when your own psychology is working against you, the humility to acknowledge what you don't know, and the discipline to stop long enough to think clearly when everyone around you is demanding immediate action.

Welcome to the reality of leadership in a chaotic world. It's not pretty, it's not always fair, and it definitely isn't what they taught you in business school.

But it's real. And real is what you need when everything is falling apart.

CHAPTER 1
IN THE BEGINNING...

Leadership. A word that is as old as time itself. The techniques are as plentiful as the years of its existence. Want to be a good leader? Then lead by example. Want to be a better leader? Incorporate your team by being supportive and understanding. Help them help you. How many times have you heard the phrase, "great leaders lead?" But what is it that great leaders do? They solve problems. Have an issue that you can't solve? Go to the leader.

At first, we are all taught to follow the leader. From conception to death, we are told what to do, how to behave, and how to act. As an infant, you're taught to follow and behave towards your parents. They teach you right from wrong. School is a series of follow-the-leaders. In our work lives, we often follow our bosses' lead. Whatever the boss says, we follow their direction. If you have a problem, you take it to the boss to have it solved. Why? Because we were taught to follow the leader.

Throughout my 40+ years of experience, which includes a career with the NYPD, I was trained and certified as both a hostage negotiator and an emergency psychological technician. My time with the hostage negotiation team taught me, maybe more than I wanted to know, about human behavior, and also laid the groundwork for what was to come. I got to understand the complexities of how and why leaders made their decisions. I learned that you really need to get into the weeds to truly understand an issue.

In 1996, Mayor Rudy Giuliani took emergency management away from the NYPD and created a mayoral agency, the Office of Emergency Management (OEM). I was asked to go to OEM, where I was ultimately appointed as the Director of Security and Intelligence Operations. Our mission focused on examining attack methodologies worldwide. Identify what groups were responsible for or claimed to take responsibility. We would then try to see if they had operational capacity in the Tristate area.

Our mission wasn't investigatory in nature; we weren't chasing the bad actors, 'Tangos,' but instead getting ahead of threats, preparing for the effects of a possible attack, and allocating resources for mitigation.

As a result of my training, experience, and roles in the intelligence world, I have been involved in situations, both in real life and in exercises, where significant efforts have been made to plan and deploy resources to prevent major terrorist attacks. Yet there were moments when I said to myself, "If the public only knew what was happening, they would be scared silly." However, somehow things always worked out despite the apparent stupidity. As we will see later in this book, it ranged from people who could not make a decision on their own, to rushing a decision to look good in front of the boss, to covering up their incompetence by overreacting and causing economic turmoil.

How many times have we been in situations where we sat around, looked at each other, and said "WTF"? Who thought of this? What were they thinking? How many of us questioned the lack of common sense when we saw something and said, "Here is a great 'Darwin Award' candidate"? This book highlights some of those moments when we looked and shook our heads in disbelief. It is the leadership lessons learned from these events that make us better than before.

In the intelligence community, we do things differently from the rest of the world. We're trained to think differently. Our thinking follows a careful, logical process that produces reliable outcomes. What if you, too, could use the same collection, analysis, and predictive methods we use to gain an advantage at work and in life? What if you had a simple, effective technique you could use again and again to help assess risk, make better decisions, and become a better leader?

Traditional leadership training focuses on the mechanics of the role. Countless books claim to build great leaders by sharing age-old nuggets of wisdom: lead by example, communicate clearly, think strategically, and delegate efficiently. These are valuable skills, no question. But what a lot of them miss is the psychological aspect of leadership, the mental battlefield where decisions are actually made. When external pressures mount, when stakeholders demand immediate answers, when the board wants results yesterday, even the best-trained leaders can crack. These pressures don't just challenge your decision-making ability; they fundamentally alter how your brain processes information. Under stress, we default to shortcuts, to gut reactions, to solutions that feel urgent rather than right. We make choices to relieve our own anxiety instead of solving the actual problem. Understanding this psychological dimension, recognizing when pressure is driving you toward hasty solutions and knee-jerk responses, is what separates leaders who merely survive from those who consistently make sound decisions under fire.

If you're in a leadership position, no matter what the size of the organization, this book is for you. I like to think of it as a shortcut for identifying potential problems before they arise and for solving those already present.

Throughout my extensive career, I have received more exceptional training than I can begin to count. I've also had the honor of providing training to others. I've taught countless courses on major case investigation, terrorism preparedness, crisis and consequence management, situational awareness, and executive protection. Now, I'm going to teach you an easy-to-use methodology that will help you become a more effective leader.

Before I dive deeper into my career journey and the lessons that shaped me, I want to give you a glimpse of where all this is heading. The technique I'll be teaching you didn't emerge from theory or academic study; it was born from practical necessity, from years of watching decisions go sideways and asking myself why.

The "STOP Technique," as I came to call it, is a simple yet powerful method that works in almost every situation, both at work and in life. It's especially valuable for leaders who are so focused on the goal that they overlook the pitfalls and liabilities along the way. Throughout this book, you'll see how the technique was applied, or should have been applied, in real-life situations, from brilliant crisis management to spectacular "Darwin Award" failures.

I'll explain the full "STOP" Technique methodology later in the book, but for now, understand this: the experiences I'm about to share, from the streets of the Bronx to the chaos of Intelligence operations, are what taught me to see the patterns that most leaders miss. Each chapter reveals another layer of how this approach developed and why it works.

Since entering the intelligence world, friends and family often ask, if you know something bad is going to happen, can you call me? I always said, sure, I'll put you on the list. But after a while, that list became too long, so I borrowed a line from the explosive ordinance folks and came up with, "If you see me running, try to keep up." Hopefully, after reading this book, you won't have as many chances to feel like you need to go for a run and be a better leader because of it.

....

Leadership Principles:

- Pressure hijacks judgment. Leaders fail when they make decisions to relieve their own anxiety rather than solve the actual problem.

- Self-awareness under stress separates effective leaders from those who merely survive.

PART 1

BAPTISM BY FIRE, HOW I LEARNED TO SEE FAILURE

CHAPTER 2
THE DAY I REALIZED
I HAD HAD ENOUGH

My entry into the world of intelligence operations was a surprise. Not a career goal, not something I had considered, and while I occasionally enjoyed them, I'm not even a huge fan of James Bond movies. I chose my career in the fourth grade when I came home to tell my mother I wanted to be a "cop" when I grew up. By the sixth grade, I started to refine my goal. I wanted to be a Homicide Detective. For the next twelve years, I dedicated myself to a raw passion that, at times, became all too consuming. Nothing was going to stop me; the career choice had been made, and learning started at that moment. I would read, study, and research as if I were writing a doctoral thesis about police work. I made friends with Police Officers and spent hours talking to them about the job.

In 1982, my dream became a reality when I was sworn in as a recruit to the New York City Police Department. I couldn't have been more prepared. I attended John Jay College of Criminal Justice in New York and spent hours in the library studying the only copy of the NYPD Patrol Guide. I wanted to minor in law, so I took all the law and police science classes offered. Friends took me to the gun range, and I became a good shot. I had the tactics down pat. Physically, I was an athlete in high school, so the gym portion was something I could handle without breaking a sweat. There was really nothing in the academy I hadn't seen, read, shot, or tried. I was ready. I graduated from the academy and was assigned to the 44th Police Precinct in the South Bronx. Some of you will be familiar with Yankee Stadium; the precinct covers this area. Here, I would work patrol in uniform and spend two years in the anti-crime unit. It is here you dress like a bum and try to make robbery arrests on the street. The following two years were spent in Robbery investigations, also in the 44th Precinct. Then it was off to become a Detective. I was sent to a command just north of Yankee Stadium.

The 46th Pct. Detective Squad room is in the middle of the South Bronx in New York City. Describing this place is not hard. It was a shit hole. Pure and simple. I always said that if you wanted to give the world an enema, this is where you would stick the hose. The office was large by department standards. We had a squad room with five desks, a small kitchen equipped with a refrigerator, stove, and a cafeteria-style table with six mismatched chairs, a bunk room with three bunk beds, and a couple of offices for the bosses. Clearly decorated from the funky, tacky era, nothing matched. The walls were painted in that sort of bluish hue, or maybe it was grey. Between the paint and the fluorescent lights, the place was depressing but an accurate reflection of the neighborhood we worked in. The area the precinct covers was rated by The New York Times as the most dangerous square mile in America. Twelve men, working in three teams, cover the detective squad, with a yearly caseload of close to 90 homicides and 4,000 almost-homicides; we were busy. Hell, if you got shot in this command and weren't expected to die, I wouldn't leave my desk to visit. The paperwork alone could choke a horse with all the forms to type out. Yes, I said 'type'; you see, it's 1987, and the department has just entered the technology implementation phase. We acquired honest-to-goodness electric typewriters to replace the old manual typewriters. We got rid of the carbon paper and replaced it with forms that had it built in. We even got a fax machine, although there was only one for the entire precinct. However, it saved a Detective from having to hand-deliver a report, known as a "49," to the bosses at the Borough office.

A detective squad room has a peculiar aura. It had that "off limits to anyone but a Detective" feel to it. Patrol cops didn't feel welcome because we made them feel that way. Those who didn't get it right away were told flat out. Before they enter, they knock. No one walks right in. Not even bosses. It was an aura we perpetrated. Don't let anyone get comfortable here. It was understood that the door was never locked when we were in, yet people still knocked. The only other room in the entire command that held such reverence was the Commanding Officer's office, and even he knocked.

In the ghetto, there is a certain hum to the environment. It is a cacophony of children playing, music blaring between salsa and reggae, and the occasional screaming followed by loud gunshots. Sometimes we didn't even have to drive to the shooting scene.

Working homicide cases here takes its toll. It must. Seeing the inhumanity between men, the depths people will go to hurt and maim each other is at first startling. Sociologists have long sought to determine its cause. Poverty, despair, lack of a structured family support system, the welfare system... who really knows? You quickly get to the point where you stand there, looking over the body of one drug dealer shot by another, lying in the gutter. It's 3 am, and the temperature is about 10 freaking degrees cold. As he bleeds out into a sewer, you realize you are the only person who, at that moment, cares. You learn without an effective defensive barrier, you will go out of your fucking mind, so you develop a thicker skin.

As for true victims, well, infants and young children are about all that's left. During my six years with the command, I handled many cases involving children. Those cases touch even the most hardened law enforcement officer. I know. It happened to me.

It started with a lady who roasted, albeit accidentally, her infant daughter.

It was early one cold winter morning. The sun was up, and there was a stillness in the air. The kind you get when it is just too damn cold to move.

The wind chill was about 15 degrees; the wind was blowing constantly, with gusts strong enough to almost knock you over. Tom Lambert and I are working the day shift. Tom is the senior Detective who had been assigned to the command years before I got there. We would develop a close relationship both as partners and friends. So close in fact, he was the best man at my wedding.

At around 9:30 am, I answered a call from a patrol unit at the Lincoln Hospital Emergency Room. The Officers reported they had a small infant, deceased, who had an extremely high body temperature. How high? Over one hundred and fifteen degrees.

"What happened? What's the back story?"

"Baby was brought in by her mother and boyfriend. Something is not right. Can you come down?"

"We are on the way."

I drove to the hospital with Lambert, where we found the mother and the Officers. The Doctor is a young resident. He is about 5'5 "tall, with greasy, short black hair, glasses, and a skinny build. He is wearing green scrubs and white sneakers. That ever-present stethoscope hangs around his neck. His speech cadence is short, quick bursts. He has more important things to do than to explain the situation to me. I'm going to give it a shot anyway. After introducing ourselves, he begins telling us what he wants us to know.

"This might be some sort of rare disease that causes very high fevers."

"Is it contagious?"

"We are testing right now. The Health Department has been notified. CDC will be next. We very well can have a health crisis on our hands."

He turns and walks away. I guess he is duty-bound to save the world today.

Tom and I walk over to the mother and boyfriend. She is in her mid-twenties, of average height, and slender. She does not appear to have any of the traits, i.e., signs of drug use or abuse, or intoxication, or mental conditions we have come to expect from residents in this area. She is sitting on a bench outside the Emergency Room door. We asked her to step into a private room to chat. The boyfriend is supportive of her, helping her stand up and assisting her to the room. He, too, is unassuming and lacks the traits we would have expected. He is polite, well-spoken, and dressed in jeans, sneakers, and a sweatshirt. While a problem for many of the people we interacted with, neither of them had any hygiene issues for us to contend with. There was nothing in our first interaction that would have led us to form a bad impression. We introduce ourselves to both. We asked the boyfriend to step ç

"So, Mom, I'm Detective Lifrieri, and this is Detective Lambert. Can you tell us what happened this morning?"

"My baby was sleeping in the crib, next to the radiator. I fed her, burped her, changed her diaper, and put her pajamas on. Then I put her to bed. When I looked at her this morning, she didn't look right. She had these dark marks around her lips and no color."

"What time did you feed her last night?"

"About eight."

Lambert offers up the next question.

"So then what happens this morning?"

"I went to check on her. She had those marks I told you. I panicked. I picked her up, wrapped her in a blanket, and ran outside to catch a cab. I didn't know what to do. I just panicked!"

I jump into the conversation.

"When you got into the cab, was it a livery cab or did you call for one?"

"It was a livery. I flagged it down, and we got into the car."

"Who picked the hospital, you or the cab driver?"

"My boyfriend."

"Where was he? He was with you?"

"Yes."

Lambert and I look at each other. Something isn't right about this. We step outside to talk to the boyfriend. I'm curious about where the boyfriend is in all of this. We ask him to step into a corner of the lobby for some privacy.

"Walk us through last night. What happened?"

"I spoke with her on the phone about nine o'clock.

Lambert and I have the same thought, but we won't look at each other so as not to telegraph what we are thinking. I started digging.

"So, you were home when this happened?"

"Yes. I called her to see if she wanted to come over."

"At about nine?"

"Yes. She said she had just given the baby a bath and put her to bed. She was going to put her to bed and come over."

"Did she come over?"

"Yes."

"What time did she get to your house?"

"About nine thirty."

"Alone, without the baby?"

"Yes."

"Who was watching the baby?"

He starts to shuffle his feet. His shoulders collapse as if they were under a great deal of weight.

"No one."

I start rubbing my eyes and face, even though it is still morning, and I am not physically tired.

"So, she shows up, without the baby. What time did she leave?"

"About eight."

"She showed up at nine thirty and left at about eight this morning?"

"Nine thirty last night… eight this morning."

"And no one is watching the baby?"

"No."

"But you come to the hospital with her. How did she get the baby and you together?"

"She woke up, sort of in a panic about leaving the baby home alone. She got dressed and grabbed a cab to go home."

"What time is that?"

"When she goes home?"

"Yes."

"I told you about eight."

"Where does she live?"

"Up around Fordham Road. About fifteen minutes by car from my apartment."

At this point, we know the baby, the mother, and the father came to the hospital. We know where he lives, but the location where it happened is still unclear. I press on with the questions.

"How did you two wind up together with the baby?"

"She went home. She saw what happened to the baby, wrapped it up in a blanket, and brought it to me. As soon as I saw it, I ran outside, got a cab, and we came here."

"So, she brought the baby to you, not directly to the hospital?"

"She panicked."

Lambert and I decided to go back to talk to the mother. We need to determine where she lives and gain access to the apartment. I confirm the story with the mother that we just got from the boyfriend. I asked her for the address. She gave it to me. She lives in an adjoining precinct. I asked her for the keys, and she told me she forgot them in the apartment. Basically, she is locked out. And then the unexpected happens. She begins to cry and shake all over. She is wailing, "My baby, my baby" over and over again. We thought this was a realization of what had just happened, but we were wrong. She gets control of herself briefly.

"Detective, please…. Save my baby!"

"I'm sorry, there isn't anything I can do at this point for her."

"Not her, him."

Lambert and I look at each other. The phrase "what the fuck" runs through our minds at the same time. I have to ask.

"Who him?"

"My baby boy."

"Where is he?"

"In the bedroom with her. I gave him a bottle and put him on the bed. PLEASE!"

We get the address and rush over to the apartment. When we get there, the doors are locked. We contact the building superintendent and instruct him to open the doors. He refuses. A cocky son of a bitch who had a major hard-on for cops. I was about to give him another reason to hate us.

A little supplemental force on the door, and we were in. The bedroom was in the rear of the apartment. We find the bedroom door locked, too. A quick kick to the lock and the door flies open. Immediately, we were hit with searing heat, like walking into a sauna. A king-size bed is in front of us, and the headboard is against the far wall. To the left of the bed is a crib, placed right in front of a gas heater. Next to the crib on the floor is a small child, a toddler, holding an empty juice bottle. I stopped for a moment. I take a deep breath. Slowly, I walk up to where he is lying. As I approach, he lifts his head off the floor and raises the empty juice bottle he carried in his right hand. I got down on one knee. I'm afraid to grab him for fear I may hurt him. He hands me his bottle. He speaks, as a small toddler would in that sweet baby voice.

"Juice?"

We arrest the mother, and the toddler is taken from her. As a result of this case, which got covered in the press, I developed an interest in investigating infant death cases. I had the opportunity to read, study, and discuss with Dr. Millard Bass, a renowned researcher who has conducted extensive work on Sudden Infant Death Syndrome cases. What we learned from his research was the suggested protocols to follow to help diagnose what we had in front of us at the scenes. While never one hundred percent foolproof, it helped us indicate sometimes it was an accident, sometimes it was murder. In others, there was no definitive answer, and you ended up with a Sudden Infant Death (SID) case. I believe we have made an impact on the crime-scene investigation processes that are still in use today.

Looking back, I remember too many times, standing in the Medical Examiner's office, looking at the body of an infant or small child, lying naked on a cold metal table, all of its life taken from it. As if the view is not enough, other senses are attacked the moment you enter the building. That chill in the air. It runs through your body the moment you enter the autopsy room. Formaldehyde, which is trying desperately to cover the smell of death, gags you. The whine of a circular saw cutting into bone. It only gets worse from here.

There are times you want to scream, times you want to cry, and times you want to shoot the asshole in front of you. Over time, the suppressed emotions reach their peak, and your personality changes. You become bitter, rude, and arrogant. Some Detectives adjust well. Perhaps it's because they care less or have learned to suppress it more effectively. Some create an emotional wall that can never be climbed over. I have been described as emotionally unavailable, especially by the women in my life. That may be true.

For me, the worst was lying in bed at night, afraid to close my eyes. Alone with my thoughts, those suppressed feelings are building up. Over time, night is transposed into day with self-doubt and a sense of urgency leaking out. How long before I find the killer? What did I miss that would prevent me from making the arrest just yet?

Want to know what it feels like? Let me tell you, it's drowning. You gasp for air, you thrash your arms and legs as fast as they can go, and you get nowhere. Unfortunately, these become the all too often days and nights you spend as a Homicide Detective.

As a leader, it is critical that you understand and learn your limits. After all, you are the leader of yourself first. The Marines teach this as one of the first rules of leadership, "know yourself and seek self-improvement." Essentially, it emphasizes the importance of being aware of your strengths and weaknesses and seeking feedback from trusted others. Life gets in the way sometimes, and we don't always see the forest for the trees. But sometimes, you encounter a person who is a great leader who looks out for you and makes not just that moment in time better, but also provides a launching pad for the rest of your career. I was fortunate enough to meet someone whom I will describe in the next chapter, without whom my career would never have reached the point it is today.

Looking back, I realized that I was learning lessons I hadn't even recognized. I was fortunate to make the right choices, though I was completely unaware of it at the time. If you're lucky like me, you make the choices, and they turn out to be the right ones. Sometimes being lucky is a good thing.

It had been six years of handling cases, many of them with children as victims. The emotional toll was too high. In the end, I was lucky; I survived. Some might think I quit, others commended me for realizing it was time to move on. In the end, I had had enough, and the time had come to move on.

My experiences over almost six years working in the squad gave me insights into life, death, and myself that I could never have achieved anywhere else. I realized a childhood dream and made it real. While I was unaware of it at the time, it would become a foundation for the rest of my career.

It doesn't matter what walk of life a person is from. They can be transient residents of impoverished neighborhoods, heads of corporations, or leaders of either the free or unfree worlds. In the end, they are all the same; they will all piss you off and frustrate you. As you progress in your career and get the opportunity to meet these leaders, the experience will be no different when dealing with their absurdities. The mother in the emergency room may have been ignorant, but she wasn't malicious. We will learn that, for political gain, some people will stop at nothing, with no remorse for whom they step on to better themselves. When you have had enough, take a deep breath and start to walk away.

Leadership Principles:

- Leaders who deny the emotional toll will make poor decisions later, as they begin making choices to reduce pain rather than solve problems.

- True leadership requires building emotional resilience while maintaining the ability to recognize when defensive barriers become walls that isolate you from effectiveness.

CHAPTER 3
THE CONVERSATION THAT CHANGED MY CAREER

The Bronx Borough Command was the kind of place that carried its own smell, coffee, ink, and weariness. The walls were an institutional beige, as if designed to drain energy rather than inspire it. The paint never quite covered the years of cigarette smoke, and even the fluorescent lights had a tired flicker, as if they'd seen too much. I'd been there countless times before, briefing chiefs and borough commanders on homicides that demanded attention, but this time felt heavier. I was called into the Bronx Chief of Detectives' office located at the Borough office to brief Chief Donald Moss. Donald Moss, big man, built like he'd once played tackle and never lost the stance. He had a calm presence, an even voice, and the kind of eyes that seemed to see more than you were saying. Most chiefs back then were known for barking orders, pounding tables, and pretending authority equaled wisdom. Moss was different. He had a stillness about him. He didn't need to bark; he made you want to listen.

I was there to talk about the murder of a little girl named Shemika Jennings.

She was nine years old, missing for three days before her body was found in the East River, stuffed into a pink laundry bag. Even now, the image comes back to me in flashes, the stillness of the river that morning, the pink fabric soaked and heavy, the way every cop on the scene went quiet when the bag was opened. There are cases you work, and then there are cases that work on you. This one had eaten away at me.

The date is September 7, 1991. I am working a 4 pm to 1 am shift in the 46th Precinct Detective Squad. My partner, Tom Lambert, is working with me. At around 10 pm, a call comes into the squad room. I answered the phone and had a very brief conversation with the caller. He is a police officer at the scene of a missing 9-year-old girl. It's 10 pm, and a little girl is missing; the family hasn't seen her all day. I'm bothered by the call and share my feelings with Tom.

Can you believe this shit?

What happened now, he replies.

Sector on scene says a 9-year-old girl is missing. The family hadn't seen her all day.

Tom shakes his head, gets up, puts on his jacket, and says Let's go.

In New York City, if a person under 10 years of age went missing, it was considered a major event. All the stops will be pulled out. We got into an unmarked police car and headed to the scene. On the way, I am vocal about my displeasure of having to go to the scene. We have experienced this numerous times. It always ended with the kid coming home after spending the night with her "friend." I'm chirping about the lack of parental control in the neighborhood. Why do we always have to come to the rescue? Tom totally ignores me, as he has heard this a thousand times and has probably said it to himself another thousand times.

When we arrive at the scene, everyone is out on the street, sitting on the building's front stoop. The weather is warm enough, as fall hasn't really kicked in yet. Not warm enough for the non-existent air conditioning in the buildings, but warm enough to sit outside at 10 pm without a coat. The little girl's mother is sitting next to an older woman, who turns out to be the little girl's grandmother. She is an African American woman, approximately in her mid-to-late sixties. She is wearing a housecoat like most old-time grandmothers did. She is polite, respectful, and very eloquent. This was not what I was expecting on the way over. In a short amount of time, she and I will come to be closer to each other, and I will affectionately call her "Grandma."

During the six months it took to solve this case, she and I would meet regularly. She had a compassionate nature. She was, in every way, a Grandmother who cared for those around her, not just herself. She was trying her best to raise a family in a ghetto with limited resources. She kept the family together.

I learned that night that Shemika was being babysat by her Uncle Daryl. Her mother, Beverly, was going out with her sisters for a girls' night. Uncle Daryl is her sister's husband. Daryl volunteers to watch the kids, Shemika and her two brothers. I'm told that sometime in the morning, Shemika wakes up and goes into Uncle Daryl's room, telling him she is hungry and wants breakfast. He tells her to "go downstairs to Grandma's apartment. She has cereal."

Shemika replies, "OK, Uncle Daryl," and leaves the apartment at around 8 am.

The story then develops: the children were playing in front of the building that morning, and they decided to go to the park a few blocks away. Shemika was alone in front of the building with them, without any adult supervision. According to the family, this was never the case. She was never allowed out without an adult, but today, apparently, it was different. I talked to the kids, and they told me they were with her at the park. I call in a bloodhound to track her, and the dog takes us to the park, to the water's edge of the Harlem River. There is an indication that a picnic table had been moved closer to the fence, and brush on the other side of the fence by the seawall had been crushed as if someone had stood on it.

For six months, I worked exclusively on this case. The press was all over it, the community was upset, and to add insult to injury, another little girl had been found dead, stuffed into a cooler in Manhattan. Was there a serial killer on the loose? These were the questions I kept asking myself repeatedly. What could I do to prevent the next killing of a little kid?

In the end, I discovered that the killer wasn't a serial killer, but an underage family member. She was killed by suffocation with a pillow while her two little brothers slept near her. Due to the perpetrator's age, I cannot provide any further details about who committed the crime or why.

After the arrest, I go to see Grandma for the last time and tell her I made an arrest. There is an emotional moment when we say goodbye to each other. We both know we will probably never see each other again. As I am leaving, she tells me that she always knew I was a great Detective and that I would figure out who killed her granddaughter. Then, as I approach the door, grab the knob, and turn it to exit, she says, "I always knew you would figure it out that it was him (naming the perpetrator)." I stopped and turned around, reminiscent of Peter Falk in the Columbo Detective series.

"Wait a minute," I said. "You knew all along? "Why didn't you say something earlier?" I am incredulous, I want to scream at her, but I couldn't get the words out fast enough. Too many thoughts and emotions rushed out at once.

"Grandma, you knew what this case meant to me and how it affected me personally. Why didn't you tell me sooner?"

She stared straight into my eyes and said, "You never asked."

When the arrest finally came, six months after the initial call, it wasn't relief I felt. It was emptiness. I'd given everything I had to that case, and it took more than it gave back.

One day after the arrest, I was going to brief the Chief on the case, so he could inform the Chief of Detectives, who would then brief the Police Commissioner, who could then brief the Mayor.

Six months of false leads, dead ends, sleepless nights, and community outrage. I was running on fumes when I walked in. My head was pounding from lack of sleep, my tie felt like a noose, and the Shemika case still had its claws in me. I was ready to give him the standard rundown, timeline, suspect status, press management, the whole routine. Moss sat behind his desk, arms folded loosely, listening.

When I finished, he nodded, leaned back slightly, and asked a question that stopped me cold.

"So how are you doing?"

It wasn't the question I expected. I thought he'd want to know about the media, or the next court date, or if I needed more manpower. Instead, he just looked at me, no agenda, no checklist, like a man actually asking another man how he was.

"I'm OK," I said, quick, deflecting, trying to push the briefing forward.

He didn't bite. "I know about the case," he said quietly. "I'm asking about you. You personally. How are you doing?"

That question hit like a body shot. I can't even remember the last time someone in command asked that. In our world, you don't talk about yourself. You weren't supposed to. It wasn't the culture. You dealt with death, tragedy, chaos, and you built a wall around it. If the wall cracked, you patched it and kept moving. Talk too much about feelings, and you'd find yourself sitting in front of a department shrink explaining why you weren't suicidal. Every cop knew that. You kept it together, or at least looked like you did.

He kept watching me, waiting. There was no judgment in his face, just patience. I could've brushed him off again, said I was fine, cracked a joke, deflected. But something in his tone made me stop pretending. For reasons I couldn't explain, I decided to tell him the truth, or at least part of it.

"To be honest, Chief," I said, pointing at my head, "this is oatmeal."

He raised an eyebrow. "What's the problem?"

"I've had enough," I said flatly. "Almost six years in the Four-Six, five in the Forty-Four before that. I'm worn out. If I could get away from police work and still get a check from the department, that would be great."

The words came out before I could pull them back. Once they were out, the silence stretched between us. I half expected him to pick up the phone and call psych services, tell them to have a seat ready for me. That's usually how this went: admit you're burned out, and you're branded damaged goods. In this job, vulnerability was weakness, and weakness was career suicide.

But Moss didn't reach for the phone. He just studied me for a long moment. The fatherly expression softened even more. "You've been doing this a while," he said. "You look tired."

He was right. I was. It wasn't the kind of tired that sleep could fix. It was the kind that seeps into your bones, the kind that comes from seeing too much, caring too much, and pretending it doesn't matter. I didn't respond. There was nothing left to say.

Then he asked something that completely blindsided me. "You ever think about the Intelligence Division?"

"The what?" I said.

"The Intelligence Division," he repeated. "You ever hear of it?"

I hesitated. I'd heard whispers, rumors it was tied to Internal Affairs, maybe some kind of shadow unit for bigwigs and political favors. None of it sounded appealing. "I don't know much about it," I said carefully. "Heard it's part of IAB. Not really my thing."

He chuckled, just once. "Unofficially, it used to be called the knife and fork squad," he said. "They handle dignitary protection, like the Secret Service. The Princess comes to New York and wants to go to dinner; you escort her."

I blinked. "No shit, department has a unit that does that?"

He smiled. "That and organized crime investigations. I used to be the XO (Executive Officer) there."

It took a second to register what he was offering. This wasn't a casual suggestion; it was a lifeline.

A way out that didn't feel like quitting. I must've looked stunned because he reached for a folder on his desk and started flipping through some papers.

"Let me make a call," he said. "Get you an application."

For a few seconds, I sat there, trying to process what was happening. I came into that office ready to talk about a homicide and maybe admit I was done. I expected a reprimand, a lecture, perhaps a referral to a therapist. Instead, he opened a door. Not because I'd dazzled him with brilliance, but because he saw I was drowning. And instead of letting me sink, he gave me a way out.

When I left his office, I walked down the hall more slowly than usual. My head was spinning, but not from fatigue. For the first time in months, maybe years, I felt something close to relief. The noise in my head, the endless churn of cases, victims, and paperwork, quieted just a little.

I stopped near the end of the corridor, staring out the window at the Bronx skyline. The city looked different from up there. You could see the grit of it all, the order behind the chaos. Maybe that's what Moss had seen in me: not burnout, but readiness for something else. Perhaps I'd been too close to the street for too long to realize it.

I thought about everything I'd said, "If I can get away from police work and still get a check." I'd meant it as a joke, but there was truth buried in it. I didn't want out of the job; I wanted out of the part that was killing me. The cases that bled into your dreams. The nights when you'd lie awake replaying every bad decision. I didn't need to escape the department; I needed to breathe again.

That conversation changed everything.

I didn't know it yet, but that was the day my career took a pivotal turn. A simple question, "How are you doing?" had pulled me off a path that would've eaten me alive. I'd walked in as a homicide detective running on fumes and walked out with the first spark of something new.

And the strangest part? Moss never made it sound like a rescue. He made it sound like leadership.

In the hours after that meeting, I couldn't shake the feeling that something fundamental had shifted. On paper, it was just a conversation between a detective and his boss. But it wasn't about paper. It was about timing, awareness, and empathy in a place that prided itself on suppressing all three.

I sat in my car outside Borough Command for a while before driving off. The usual chaos of the Bronx played out around me, sirens in the distance, kids yelling on the corner, the simultaneous screeching of tires and racing of the engine of the sanitation truck rolling by. Normally, that soundtrack ran through me like static, but that day it was muffled. Moss's voice kept echoing: How are you doing? Not the words themselves, but the way he said them, without judgment, without expectation, just curiosity.

Most people think leadership in law enforcement is about authority. They think it's about making decisions fast, giving orders, and keeping the machine running. That's part of it, but the more challenging part, the part few get right, is noticing the human being inside the uniform. Moss did. In a world where most leaders asked what I was doing, he asked how I was doing.

I didn't know it then, but that single act would rewire how I saw leadership for the rest of my life.

That night, I went home and sat in the kitchen long after my wife went to bed. I poured a drink, opened the case file for the Shemika Jennings homicide, and just stared at it. The kid's photo looked back at me, nine years old, eyes bright, smile wide, a kid who'd never gotten to grow up. I closed the file and slid it into a box with the others. Usually, I'd leave a case open in my mind for weeks, even after it was closed on paper. But this time, I didn't. Maybe I was done. Maybe Moss had given me permission to be done.

The truth is, I was exhausted in ways the department didn't measure. You can chart arrests, case closures, overtime hours, but not the erosion of your own humanity. Each scene, each victim, takes something from you, and you start trading pieces of yourself just to keep functioning. Some detectives hold on; others turn cynical. I was caught somewhere in between.

In the weeks that followed, I completed the transfer paperwork that Moss had arranged. It was surreal to write my own exit from a world that had defined me since I was a kid. My hands actually shook when I typed the request for reassignment, not from fear, maybe relief. It's strange how leaving something you love can feel like a survival instinct.

I never told Moss how much that conversation meant. Maybe I figured he already knew. Guys like him didn't do things for thanks; they did them because it was the right thing to do. Years later, I'd come to realize how rare that was, leadership that acts quietly, without credit, in the cracks between policy and humanity.

For weeks after, I replayed our talk in my head. The rhythm of it. The way he listened. The moment he offered me Intelligence, like he'd been saving that option for someone who actually needed it. He didn't see weakness in my fatigue; he saw potential in the space behind it. That distinction is everything.

When people burn out, the easy move is to replace them. The harder, wiser move is to redirect them. Moss did that instinctively. He saw something I couldn't, what I might still have to give if I wasn't crushed by the weight of what I'd already given.

That's leadership. Not standing at the podium or yelling orders across a room. Leadership is pulling one person back from the edge without making a scene. It's noticing when someone's fire is flickering and cupping your hand around it so it doesn't go out.

A few days after the transfer, I went back to the squad to clean out my locker. The guys didn't know what to make of it. Some assumed I was getting promoted; others thought I'd pissed someone off. The truth was less dramatic but more complicated. I'd reached the end of what homicide could teach me. The rest of my lessons would have to come from somewhere else.

The 46th Precinct squad room looked the same, dim lights, chipped desks, that familiar smell of burnt coffee and exhaustion. But standing there with an empty locker, I felt detached, as if I were visiting my own past. These walls had shaped me, hardened me, and now they were letting me go.

I left the building without looking back. Outside, the air was sharp and cold, the kind of wind that wakes you up. For the first time in years, I didn't have a case waiting for me. I didn't have a stack of 49s to write or witnesses to chase. I had nothing but uncertainty, and for once, that felt like freedom.

Moss's office had been a quiet room on a noisy day. That's what leadership can do, it stills the noise long enough for someone to hear themselves think. Most of us never get that moment. We push through burnout, mistaking endurance for strength, when what we need is direction.

I learned more from that five-minute conversation than I had from a decade of roll calls and command memos. Not because he said something profound, but because he listened. He didn't fix me; he gave me a choice.

Looking back, I realize how easily that day could have gone the other way. If Moss had been the type to lecture or dismiss, I would've walked out, buried the exhaustion, and kept grinding until something broke, my health, or maybe worse. Instead, he saw that burnout wasn't failure. It was a transition.

That's the part most leaders miss. When someone says they've had enough, it's not always defeat; it might be evolution. It's the body and mind's way of saying, you've learned everything you can here; it's time to grow somewhere else.

Years later, when I found myself in leadership roles, I carried that lesson with me. Every time someone came into my office looking drained or disillusioned, I heard Moss's voice in my head: How are you doing? It's such a simple question, but it demands courage on both sides, courage to ask and courage to answer honestly.

You can't fake that kind of conversation. People can tell the difference between checking a box and genuinely caring. The difference is everything.

When I finally received the call that my transfer to Intelligence had been approved, I drove to work that morning with a strange mix of nerves and hope. I didn't know what was coming next, but I knew it would be different. Moss had opened a door I didn't even know existed.

I will never forget that. And even decades later, through the chaos of intelligence work, through crisis management, through the politics and egos and pressure, I always think back to that office in the Bronx. One question. One honest answer. One open door.

That day in the Bronx, Chief Donald Moss didn't promote me. He preserved me. And in doing so, he taught me what real leadership looks like.

....

Leadership Principles:

- Sometimes leadership isn't about rewarding brilliance; it's about recognizing fatigue. The best leaders open doors not because someone's at their peak, but because they see that person at the breaking point, and know that redirecting them is the only way to save their potential.

- When someone says, "I've had enough," don't write them off. They might not be quitting; they might be ready for a different kind of responsibility.

CHAPTER 4
WALKING INTO INTELLIGENCE AND FINDING CHAOS

The first thing that hit me when I walked into the NYPD Intelligence Division was how quiet it was. Not the usual quiet of professionalism, but the eerie kind, the quiet that says no one knows what the hell is going on.

I was expecting something different, something sharper. After all, this was Intelligence. You imagine a place buzzing with coordination, phones ringing off the hook, walls covered with maps and classified briefings, men and women moving with purpose. Instead, I stepped into what looked like the waiting room of a dentist's office that had given up on itself.

The division was located in a commercial office building on Hudson Street in Tribeca, the same type of glass-and-steel structure that housed insurance companies and real estate firms. I remember thinking, This can't be it: no precinct smell, no echo of radios, no one yelling for backup or coffee. The lobby had potted plants, fluorescent lights, and a single reception desk guarded by a man who looked like he'd been sitting there since electricity was invented.

I walked past him and took the elevator up to the fourth floor. Walking down the hall, I noticed the names of several companies engraved on metal plates, affixed to the door. I was looking for room 401. When I arrived, I noticed there was no name on the door, only a number.

I wasn't sure whether to knock or go right in. I take a breath, open the door, and let myself in. Sitting at what can be described as a large reception desk is a male, pale, thin individual with greasy blond hair that sticks up in the back and glasses that magnify his eyes just enough to make him look perpetually surprised. This was the first "intelligence officer" I met. I called him Sparky.

"Can I help you?" he said flatly, not looking up from his newspaper.

"Yeah," I said, still standing with my bag in hand. "Detective Lifrieri. I've been assigned here as of today."

He blinked once, unimpressed. "Wonderful. Congratulations."

The way he said it, you could tell he didn't mean a word.

"Do you know who I'm supposed to report to?"

He shrugged. "Didn't know you were coming. Nobody told me."

That was my welcome to the NYPD Intelligence Division, an agency that prided itself on knowing everything but somehow didn't know I existed.

I waited at the desk for someone to claim me, but no one did. Phones rang, people passed by in plain clothes, and nobody stopped. It felt like walking into a secret club where everyone speaks a language you don't.

Eventually, a lieutenant appeared, short and energetic, "Detective Lifrieri? I'm Lieutenant Morales. Sorry for the confusion, they never tell us when someone's assigned. Let's get you settled."

She gave me a polite smile, the kind reserved for guests you didn't invite but had to entertain. I followed her through a maze of hallways, each one lined with closed doors and frosted windows. Behind every door, muffled voices and the clack of typewriter keys. No laughter. No energy. Just bureaucracy and secrets.

After some paperwork and a short introduction to clerical staff who looked at me like an intruder, Morales told me to hang tight in reception until they figured out where I belonged. So, I sat there, watching Sparky shuffle papers and taking the occasional phone call.

The minutes stretched into hours. I read an old copy of Newsweek from the reception table, then another. Nobody came for me. Around noon, I bought a sandwich from the street vendor outside and ate it back at my post like a kid left behind on a field trip.

By the time the afternoon rolled around, I realized nobody was coming. This was my first day in Intelligence, and I was forgotten by the very people who were supposed to know everything.

That was my introduction to "secrecy."

By the second day, I started to see the pattern. The division operated in silence, maintaining plausible deniability. Everyone had a project, nobody talked about it, and most didn't seem to know what the others were doing. Doors that weren't locked were guarded by stares that might as well have been.

I asked Sparky who I should report to. He didn't even look up from his desk. "Someone will tell you."

They didn't.

By now, I had turned into part of the furniture. I answered phones, read the newspaper, and pretended to be busy. At one point, Morales stopped by again, shaking her head. "I swear, Detective, they never tell us anything. It's all classified."

I laughed. "Classified from who? Me?"

She gave me a look that said exactly.

Later that day, I called my wife. "So, how's the new assignment?" she asked.

"This place is so secret," I said, "they won't even tell me what I'm doing."

On the third morning, Sparky waved me down as I walked in. "The Chief wants to see you."

I followed him down a narrow hallway to a corner office with frosted glass and no nameplate. Inside, sitting behind a heavy wooden desk, was a man who could've been pulled straight from a 1970s cop show. He had gray hair, wore a cardigan that looked like something Mr. Rogers would wear, and held a coffee mug like it was part of his hand.

"Chief," Sparky said, gesturing to me. "Detective Lifrieri."

The Chief looked up, eyes narrowing like he was focusing a camera lens. "What parachute did you fly in on?"

I froze. Was that an actual question? "Sir?"

"Who dropped you here?"

"I was transferred," I said. "Orders came from the Chief of Detectives' office."

He grunted, unimpressed, and went back to stirring his coffee. After a long pause, he said, "What do you know about Russians?"

I hesitated. I wasn't sure if this was a test or a joke. So, I gave the first answer that came to mind.

"They make a great vodka."

He stared at me without blinking. The silence hung so long it started to vibrate. Finally, he nodded once, almost to himself. "Good," he said. "You're working reception, midnights. There's a closet next to the desk, with a phone inside. If it rings, answer it."

That was it. No explanation, no context. Just a sentence that sounded like something from a bad spy movie.

I walked out wondering if this was a punishment, a test, or both.

The midnight shift at Intelligence was exactly as miserable as it sounded.

The building was empty, except for a few night staff members and me, sitting at a desk under the hum of fluorescent lights, waiting for that phone in the closet to ring, but it never did. I later learned that that was the Chiefs' way of making sure you stayed awake. He thought if he told you it might ring, it might be him calling, and God forbid you missed that call. It was like being a child, afraid, but the difference was that we were supposed to be adults. Maybe all of us were, except him.

I'd patrol the floor, peek into the darkened offices, and wonder what the hell I was doing there.

Sometimes, I'd stare at the closet phone and imagine it ringing, some secret call that would finally make sense. It never did.

By the third night, I was convinced this assignment was the Chiefs' way of hazing me for cracking a vodka joke.

At 7 a.m., Sparky came in for his shift and mumbled, "Chief wants to see you."

I trudged back down the hall, expecting another cryptic riddle. The Chief was there, cardigan still on, coffee mug still in hand. Same setup, same stare.

"What do you know about Russians?" he asked again.

I blinked. Was this déjà vu or insanity?

I decided to play it differently this time. "Funny you should ask, Chief," I said, leaning into it. "I've been doing some reading, the past few nights, on the desk. It looks like Russian organized crime has been moving into the city. Serious problems, money laundering, extortion, fraud, all of it."

He nodded slowly, then set the mug down. "That's great," he said. "You're now in charge of the Russian Organized Crime Project. Start today."

I stared at him. "A Russian Organized Crime Project? What does that even mean?"

He shrugged. "We need cases on Russians. Get some started."

"Any thoughts or direction?" I asked.

"You're a detective, right? You have a criminal background, right?"

"Yes, sir."

"Then do your job. Don't make me draw you a picture."

And with that, he went back to sipping his coffee.

I walked out of his office in disbelief. In less than a week, I'd gone from forgotten rookie to night watchman to head of a "project" that didn't exist. That was Intelligence.

Later that morning, I sat back at the reception desk, trying to process what had just happened. Sparky looked up from his newspaper. "So, how'd it go?"

"I think I'm running a Russian crime unit," I said.

He grinned. "Welcome to Intel."

It didn't take long to realize how deep the dysfunction ran. The division was a paradox, people obsessed with secrecy but starved of direction. Everyone had clearance, but no one had clarity. You could walk through the halls and feel the weight of unspoken rules pressing down on you. Conversations stopped when you entered a room. Files were locked away, not because they were sensitive, but because no one trusted anyone else.

It was the kind of place that mistook confusion for importance.

Every door had a nameplate. Every nameplate meant something classified. But ask three people what the division did, and you'll get three different answers.

I'd gone from the most violent square mile in America to a unit that couldn't organize a coffee run without a clearance form.

Still, something about it fascinated me. Maybe it was the absurdity of it all, the illusion of control, the theater of secrecy. Perhaps it was the challenge. I'd spent a career surviving chaos on the streets. Now I was learning to survive chaos in a suit and tie.

And somehow, that was going to be my new reality.

The longer I sat in that office, the more I realized Intelligence wasn't about intelligence at all; it was about control. Or at least, the illusion of it. The place operated on secrecy like a drug. Everyone was addicted to knowing something others didn't, and the less they shared, the more important they felt.

In homicide, information was oxygen. You shared what you knew because someone else's insight could break a case wide open. Here, it was the opposite. People held onto data as if it were gold bullion, locking it in cabinets, whispering behind closed doors, and labeling everything classified. Half of it wasn't even worth hiding. It wasn't national security; it was insecurity.

That was my first real exposure to organizational dysfunction disguised as sophistication. The culture rewarded silence, not solutions. If you asked too many questions, you would be seen as suspicious rather than curious. The "classified" label wasn't protecting intelligence; it was protecting incompetence.

Leadership in that environment took on a strange form. Instead of guiding people, the higher-ups managed perception. They ruled through ambiguity, keeping everyone guessing and slightly afraid of being left out of the loop. I'd worked for tough bosses before, but this was something else, leadership by confusion.

I learned something that first week, a sentiment I heard before, that a leader who hides behind secrecy is just hoarding, not leading.

It wasn't all malice. Some of it was habit. When systems grow into bureaucracies, confusion becomes a survival skill. People learn to speak in circles, to nod without agreeing, and to act busy without producing anything. The irony is, the more they talked about intelligence, the less they seemed to understand what it meant.

I used to think secrecy was a sign of importance. Now I saw it for what it really was, an excuse. A shield for indecision. A curtain that kept people from realizing the guy in charge had no idea what was happening.

That morning, when the Chief told me, "You're in charge of the Russian Organized Crime Project," I didn't see the humor in it. It felt arbitrary, even reckless. However, I later recognized the deeper problem. He wasn't strategic. He was improvising, deciding not because it was right, but because it sounded decisive. In a place where chaos was constant, appearance was everything.

That's the trap leaders fall into when they don't know what's going on; they overcompensate with theater. You give orders that sound bold but mean nothing. You act confidently to cover the gaps in your understanding. You make secrecy your armor so no one can question your competence.

Sound familiar? It's not just an Intelligence problem; it's universal. I've seen it in police commands, government agencies, and corporate boardrooms. When people don't understand the "why," they stop caring about the "what." Confusion doesn't create loyalty. It creates cynicism.

I learned that lesson early in my intelligence career. I realized it by sitting at a reception desk, waiting for instructions that never came. I discovered it by answering a phone that never rang. I learned it by watching a leader mistake mystery for management.

Later in my career, when I built my own teams, I made sure that no one ever had to wonder why they were there. You want people to follow you? Give them context. Purpose doesn't come from orders; it comes from understanding what the context is.

Moss, back in the Bronx, had led with empathy. He asked questions that mattered and listened to the answers. The Chief in Intelligence led with ambiguity. He asked riddles and rewarded whoever pretended to solve them. Both men had authority, but only one inspired trust.

That contrast became one of the defining lessons of my career: leadership without clarity breeds chaos, and not the kind you can learn from.

True chaos, the kind that refines people, comes from uncertainty in the world around you. But manufactured chaos, the kind born from bad leadership, only corrodes. It makes good people defensive, makes them stop sharing, and pushes them to protect their turf rather than the mission.

Still, I couldn't ignore the irony: this was supposed to be the elite division, the best of the best. And yet, no one knew what I was doing there, least of all me.

When the Chief finally handed me the Russian Organized Crime Project, it wasn't a reward; it was an escape. He'd given me just enough rope to hang myself or prove him wrong. Either way, I was off his radar. But what he didn't realize was that chaos didn't intimidate me. I'd been living in it my whole career. The difference now was that the chaos wasn't on the street; it was behind a desk.

If the Bronx had taught me how to survive danger, Intelligence would be about learning how to survive dysfunction.

I started piecing together my new role on instinct. If no one were going to define my mission, I would define it myself. That became my coping mechanism, and eventually, my leadership philosophy. Don't stop until someone says stop. When the system gives you nothing but confusion, build your own clarity.

Because the truth is, organizations like that don't collapse from external threats; they collapse from internal indifference.

The secrecy, the whisper networks, and the arbitrary decisions weren't protecting national security. They were protecting egos. And in time, that realization would shape everything I did after.

Years later, when I built crisis teams, I reflected on those first days in Intelligence. I remembered Sparky with his newspaper, Morales trying to make sense of orders that never came, the Chief in his cardigan, sipping coffee like a man in another dimension. It would've been funny if it weren't such a perfect snapshot of what happens when leadership forgets its purpose.

Every organization, no matter how sophisticated, can rot from the top down if it stops communicating the "why."

You can survive a lack of resources. You can survive bad press. You can even survive failure. But you cannot survive confusion that masquerades as control.

That's what the Intelligence Division taught me, accidentally.

It showed me that chaos isn't the enemy; it's how leaders handle it that matters. Some use it as a cover. Others use it as fuel. The difference is honesty.

Moss had saved my career by seeing through chaos to potential. The Chief in Intelligence taught me how chaos can be weaponized to keep people small. Both lessons shaped me.

And the irony of it all? I was learning more about leadership in an organization that barely functioned than I had in years of doing actual police work.

....

Leadership Principles:

- Secrecy without purpose is not strength; it's theater. Leaders who withhold information are not protecting their organizations; They are paralyzing them in the name of maintaining control. Confusion becomes policy, and good people stop trying. Real intelligence shouldn't be hidden; it should be shared to strengthen others.

- Organizations that prioritize mystery over meaning will always confuse compliance with competence. Leaders who think silence equals power will wake up one day to find no one listening.

CHAPTER 5
THE RUSSIANS, THE BUREAU, AND THE ART OF NOT SHARING

The story didn't begin with a briefing, a lead, or a single piece of field intelligence. It started with a glossy magazine.

In January 1993, Vanity Fair published an article on the emerging problem of Russian organized crime. As the story goes, the Police Commissioner was reading the magazine. As he read the story, he reached the final few paragraphs, which stated that the elite NYPD Intelligence Bureau had no detective assigned to investigate it. Once he finishes the article, he calls the Chief of Intelligence and tells him to get something started. So, an order came down from above: *Start a Russian Organized Crime Project. Immediately.* That was the genius of the system. Real intelligence rarely moved the room, but a magazine cover did.

And that's when I come into the picture. Albeit a couple of days delayed because I attempted humor. That sense of humor didn't translate well in a division where irony was treated like insubordination.

Now, apparently, I was the one leading the department's push into Russian organized crime.

No one could tell me what that meant. There were very few case files, no informants, and no direction beyond "coordinate with the Bureau." That's how the NYPD often handled big ideas: declare a new initiative, assign a name, and hope someone figured out the details before the press hit us again.

I learned quickly that the Russians were huge into Medicare and Medicaid fraud. I met an acquaintance who was the Special Agent in Charge of the Inspector General's Office of Health and Human Services Administration in New York. Bruno Varano was a typical New Yorker. Not bashful, rather direct, very polished, and willing to roll up his sleeves to get things done. Bruno was very welcoming, understood my situation, and was willing to form a team to collaborate. It was a win-win for the two of us. By allowing me, with the NYPD's resources, to join his team, he gave them access to the technical capabilities I had from the Intelligence Division. From my perspective, this was great because within a few days, I had set up a task force with the Fed's to go after the Russians. Bruno was my kind of guy.

Bruno hand-selected a Special Agent working under him, whom I had the pleasure of working closely with, Jaysen Eisengrein. Jaysen and I worked well together.

Bruno, Jaysen, and I met to discuss the new "Task Force" we had just started, and thought the FBI should be brought in. We all agreed it was probably useless, but it would play well in the press when word got out. The FBI had a bad reputation for taking everything and giving nothing. We set up a meeting and hoped for the best.

The FBI arrived late, with the arrogance that only they could muster. Now, the NYPD has a similar reputation, and I think that is where the rub between the agencies comes from. The Bureau had cases against the Russians in both counterintelligence and organized crime. Working with our group would provide them with a treasured trove of intelligence to identify the people they had targeted.

We didn't even make it to introductions before the Bureau rep started talking about the need for "an MOU to establish parameters." An MOU (Memorandum of Understanding) is a document that outlines how the parties will collaborate.

He slid a draft across the table like a poker dealer. It said, in diplomatic language, that the Bureau would "share information as appropriate," except they couldn't share any "personally identifiable data, and ongoing subject details."

In other words: things that mattered.

Bruno looked stunned. We were looking at each other around the conference table when Jaysen finally said, "So what exactly are we sharing?"

The FBI agent gave the kind of smile that precedes an exit. "Cooperation," he said. "We're sharing cooperation."

Bruno was incredulous.

Looking directly at the FBI Agent, he says, "Personal identifying information, like social security numbers? Is that what you're including in your data that can't be shared?"

The FBI looks him straight in the eye and says, "Yes."

Being from New York and having no patience, I was ready to explode in true New York style. Bruno was a little more experienced in dealing with matters like this. He held his tongue, didn't get flustered, and told the Agent that he must have been mistaken in his understanding of information.

"You see, in the event you're not paying attention here, we are the agency that issues Social Security numbers. It's our data. We have access to it, and you want it. You're telling us that you can't share our data with us," Bruno said sarcastically, but politely.

"Yes. It is a National Security issue," was the reply from the FBI Agent.

I couldn't believe what I just heard. They contributed nothing and sought all the information. Then they tell us they can't share due to National Security. What a crock of shit.

That was the moment I realized that with them, this wasn't a task force; it was a theater.

When I returned to the office, I attempted to summarize the problem in a memo. I tried to write that the "current interagency model prioritizes information protection over operational impact." It sounded clinical, but what I meant was that this whole thing is ridiculous. We never really got to work with the FBI. I guess they had a lack of respect for us and considered us bastard children. They were real investigators handling national security issues; we were just playing "cops and robbers."

A few days later, stupidity reached its peak.

One of the few things the Intelligence Chief had told me was that I needed to establish an MOU with the FBI. This made it appear as though we had a lot going on. By visiting HHS and establishing a task force, I thought I had accomplished two goals simultaneously. Clearly, I was mistaken. We never received the MOU with the FBI for the task force.

Since I was ordered to set up an MOU with the FBI, and the task force one didn't cover it, I tried to get a point of contact (POC) from the Bureau so I could possibly play with them.

It probably took a couple of months to finalize our MOU. I had started the process, but wasn't expecting anything positive to come from it.

One day, I got a call from an FBI Special Agent assigned to Russian cases. He told me the MOU had been approved and believed the best first step would be to meet, and that he would be "willing" to go over our files and "bring them up to date." I could only imagine what was to come of this, having no trust at all in them. What came of it, I could not even fathom if you gave me a thousand tries.

This adventure starts when he asks me to meet him so I can hand over the files.

"Want to meet at my office? I ask.

No is his reply.

How about I come to your office?

No again is his reply.

He had a better idea. He wanted to meet in a coffee shop so we could blend into the surroundings.

"Blend into what?" was my reply.

Here was a guy who fancied himself as James Bond. Neither of us was undercover. We were both readily identifiable as law enforcement officers. We met at a coffee shop near the FBI Headquarters, where I am sure people from his agency were having breakfast. But I am willing to play along. Things like this give you something to talk about over dinner.

So Special Agent James Bond and I meet. I have a large envelope containing approximately 10 old, dusty case folders, stuffed into a larger manila envelope with a drawstring to keep it closed. There is nothing unusual about these, as they have been stored on a shelf. We are sitting opposite each other, and I go to hand him the folder. He puts his hand up and stops me.

"Hand it to me under the table," he says.

"Really," I say.

"Don't let anyone see what you are handing me."

Had I not been there to witness this, I would have thought it was a scene from a Leslie Nielsen film, such as Naked Gun. So, I look around to make sure no one is watching and hand the envelope under the table. He takes it and places it on the floor by his feet. The thought crosses my mind; how funny would it be if James Bond left it behind?

A few weeks go by, and there are no updates from him. I decided to call to ask whether there is any progress on the files.

"I have about six of them ready for you. Do you want to meet and pick them up or wait until they are all done?"

Curiosity was killing me.

"Let's meet, I'm interested to see what you have."

We arranged another surreptitious meeting at the same coffee shop. This time, he hands me the envelope under the table. It appears thinner to my touch, so I know I'm only going to get what he said I would. I am eager to return to my office to review the updates made to the files.

The moment I get back to my office at Intel, I don't even take a seat at my desk. I set the envelope down and untied the very tight knot in the string around it. Contemplating cutting it out of sheer frustration, I finally untie it. As he promised, there were six old case folders. The same ones I gave him, a little less dust. Anxiously, I pull the first one out, not looking for any particular file.

What I saw shocked me so much that I fell back into my chair. What happened to the file that caused this reaction? Let me explain.

I opened the file and pulled a form that required you to fill in the blanks: name, address, city, state, and zip code. It also asked for Personal Identifying information, such as DOB, Social Security numbers, other names the subject of the investigation had used (AKA), phone numbers used, and similar information.

What I saw were holes through the sheet of paper, not from insects, but from Special Agent James Bond's hand. He actually cut AKA's and phone numbers out of *MY FILES*! Apparently, he had a special skill in paper-cutting that no one knew about. If he had added a few folds, it would have qualified as *KIRIGAMI*. A Japanese art form that involves cutting and folding paper, similar to paper cutting, but with additional folding.

I have very little patience for most things I encounter in life. I am not known for my patience or for pausing quickly enough to think before I speak. As I get older, it becomes increasingly difficult to press that button down. This was no exception.

Sitting and stewing over the fact that he dared to redact my files, I decided to call him. For what came next, I must give him some credit.

I picked up the phone and called him. He must have expected the call because he picked it up on the first ring. As soon as he answered, I said his name and then went on a soliloquy that would have made a grizzled old truck driver blush.

He remained calm, spoke in even tones, and remained professional.

"Sal, you need to understand that the information we cut out is for National Security reasons."

My response was quick, "bullshit."

He continues, "The information we took out has to do with National Security, and I cannot explain any further."

Once again, being eloquent, I say "bullshit."

"I don't know how much more I can explain. You can't have that information."

I'm now yo-yoing between sitting and standing. I started to get stares from the others around me. No one at Intel ever raises their voice. No one was ever passionate about anything. It was like they were on medications given at psychiatric hospitals. Here I am, screaming at the FBI. Had they had any interest in life, they should have started a pool to see how long I would last in Intel. Even I might have taken that bet.

The call ends with me winded and an almost-broken handset back in its cradle. Now I have to determine what's next, but not regarding the case. No, that would be straightforward. I had to figure out how to screw with this bullshit. I gave it some thought for a few minutes and developed a plan that some might say was diabolical. I called him back.

This time, the phone rang several times. He must have considered whether he would pick it up, but eventually he did.

I start by saying, "Listen, I want to apologize for what just happened. That was totally unprofessional, and I should never have done that. Please accept my apology."

Graciously, he accepts. Now comes the fun part as I continue.

"You have to understand that I am just a ghetto cop who is unfamiliar with dealing at your level. It took me a bit to think this through, but I now know what you did. You were sending me a message. I got it loud and clear. Thank you."

Now he is becoming somewhat worried. I can hear it in his voice.

"What are you talking about? What message? I'm not sending any message here."

My turn to remain calm and professional, the intensity building in his voice. He is starting to lose it, and I'm enjoying every freaking minute of it.

"Agent Bond, I know what you did. You showed me how to send a message without breaking the rules. I just wanted to let you know I am sorry for what happened before and to thank you for the message."

Now I can only picture him standing at his desk, getting increasingly loud on the phone. Panic is starting to set in.

"Listen, I don't know what you are talking about. I didn't send any cryptic message, and I didn't share any secrets with you. I told you, you can't have that intel on those people. That's why I cut it out; that's National Security information."

He is almost where I want him.

"James, I understand, you can't tell me, but the message was loud and clear. Thank you."

Now I've got him, screaming on his end. Payback's a bitch. I let him rant for a bit. Fairplay, I figure. Then I dropped the grenade.

'James, you couldn't tell me for National Security reasons. I got it. However, by excluding the information in the files, I know what information is good and what is not. The phone numbers you have cut out, you have wiretapped. The associate names you cut are under active surveillance. This is brilliant. I have to hand it to you. You provided me with current, active information without compromising National Security. I love this."

If you could hear someone swallow their tongue on the phone, this was probably the time.

"You have no idea what is active or what is current information. How do you think you can make that assessment?"

My response ends the call abruptly.

"Because I have a copy of the files. When I placed your sheet over mine, the holes you created allowed information from the bottom sheet to pass through. Ergo to wit, I know what you couldn't say verbally, and to that I say thank you again!"

Now was the time for his handset to break into pieces. I sat down in my chair and smiled. The guys around me looked at me like they were afraid. How did this lunatic go from screaming to smiling in all of about 10 minutes? Welcome to police work fellows. Sometimes you play good cop, and someone plays bad cop. Sometimes, you get to play both parts yourself.

It didn't take long for the repercussions to hit. I expected something. Probably a written reprimand, or a command discipline in which they take four hours of your vacation time as punishment. I didn't think it was an executable offense. No one in the department liked the Bureau. They never played nicely with anyone. Publicly, I would get smacked, and privately, I would get a pat on the back. Or that was what I expected.

It took about twenty minutes for my phone to ring. The Chiefs' clerk called my desk.

"Detective, the Chief wants to see you now. Right now."

"I'm on my way up now."

Before I leave my desk, I take a sheet of paper from the redacted file. Better to be prepared and have at least a reason for what I did. Maybe he would at least appreciate the passion. But I knew he had no sense of humor.

I get to the third floor and knock on the door. Same Chief when I got to the command. Same Mr. Rogers sweater. Same coffee cup in his hand. He is sitting behind his desk with the same sense of humor.

"Chief, you called for me?"

"Get in here, now."

This is not off to a good start. My hostage negotiation team training kicks in. Let him speak; determine the issue. Listen first, don't get defensive.

He goes on a rant that was somewhat respectable. I never say a word. I stand there, in front of his desk, taking the shots. His questions are rapid fire, no time for rebuttal.

"Didn't I tell you to set up an MOU with the bureau? Didn't I tell you to play nicely with them? Why did I get a call from the Assistant Director saying that you played fuck around with his guy? What is the secret message you got? Are you out of your mind?

I tried to think about responses. Instead, without saying a word, I held up the piece of paper from the file, the one with the holes. He stops for a second and looks at it.

"That's our file, right?"

I merely nod, not uttering a single word, and still holding the page up in front of him.

"What are all the holes? Did they do that?"

I nod again, still not saying a word.

"They cut our files up and told us they can't share with us our own information?"

Once again, I nod.

He is getting increasingly animated.

"National Security, my ass. What kind of idiot is he? Jesus Christ, they cut up our own homework and call it national security."

I was tempted to explain, but thought better of it. I just shrugged my shoulders.

Without me saying a word, he throws me out of the office. Funny thing, I never heard about that again.

That was my education in the art of not sharing. I was studying the anatomy of dysfunction. I started asking myself how an agency full of competent people could consistently make incompetent decisions. It wasn't laziness. It wasn't malice. It was something more profound, cultural rot disguised as procedure.

The Bureau calls it security. City Hall calls it oversight. The lawyers call it compliance. Whatever name you gave it, the effect was the same: paralysis presented as professionalism. Everyone wanted to look serious; no one wanted to look wrong, and in that space between pride and fear, leadership died.

I realized that secrecy had become a performance art. It wasn't about protecting information; it was about safeguarding status. When people fear being exposed, they start wrapping everything in classified tape until nothing moves.

That's when I learned the first hard truth of intelligence work: when you hear someone say "you don't need to know," what they really mean is "I don't want to explain."

I saw the same pathology replicated in new costumes later in emergency management and private-sector consulting. Instead of "classified," the word was "proprietary." Instead of national security, it was brand security. The intent was identical: to limit access, centralize authority, and keep the circle small so that blame stayed small.

When I worked at OEM, the fight wasn't over mobsters; it was over radio frequencies, response jurisdiction, and who got to talk to the mayor first. Every agency sought to lead, but no one sought to cooperate. During one interagency briefing, I joked that if a bomb detonated, the most significant casualty would be the chain of command. No one laughed, but everyone knew I was correct.

Leadership failure is never about a lack of intelligence; it's about the misuse of it. Systems collapse not because people are stupid, but because they're scared. Scared of losing credit, afraid of being replaced, terrified of being the one to say this isn't working. The irony is that by protecting their relevance, they destroy their value.

As I built my own company years later, I tried to create the opposite culture. At PCC Secure, I wanted people to question everything, to explain their reasoning, to treat "why" as a requirement, not an insult. Because I'd seen what happens when organizations let secrecy masquerade as competence, it breeds ignorance and passes it off as leadership.

Real leaders explain. Real leaders teach. Real leaders accept that once others understand what they do, they may no longer be the most important person in the room, and they're okay with that.

In every bureaucracy I've worked in, from NYPD to Homeland Security to private clients, the ones who failed the hardest were those who confused silence with strength. They mistook holding information for holding power.

If you ever want to test an organization's integrity, ask for information that crosses departmental lines. The reaction will tell you everything. If they start citing legal clauses and jurisdiction, you're in a defensive culture. If they begin explaining context and implications, you're in a learning one.

That's the hidden lesson behind the Russians and the Bureau. It wasn't an interagency feud; it was a mirror. It showed us how systems built on fear can't produce leadership. They can only produce hierarchy.

Years later, I'd watch corporate executives make the same mistake during crisis response drills. They'd withhold details "for optics," or delay updates "until PR signs off." Every second of silence widened the gap between perception and reality, and by the time truth caught up, credibility was gone.

The difference between operational failure and leadership failure is subtle but lethal. Operational failure happens when things go wrong. Leadership failure occurs when no one is allowed to say they already have.

That Russian project taught me one thing I've carried since: information is the oxygen of leadership. Cut it off, and even the most innovative team suffocates.

Every organization has its Bureau, the department or person who guards information as currency. The language changes, but the behavior doesn't. Leaders who hide behind classification, confidentiality, or policy aren't protecting their mission; they're protecting their ego.

If you ever find yourself leading through chaos, remember this: the only thing more dangerous than bad intelligence is good intelligence locked away by people who can't admit they need help.

Leadership Principles

- Information is the Oxygen of Leadership - Hoarding information doesn't protect an organization; it suffocates it. When leaders treat information as personal currency or hide behind classifications like "national security," "proprietary," or "need to know," they're often protecting their ego rather than their mission.

- The gap between perception and reality widens with every second of silence driven by protecting optics rather than addressing truth.

PART 2
WE ARE SAFE IN SPITE OF OURSELVES

CHAPTER 6
BUILDING EMERGENCY MANAGEMENT IN A CITY THAT DIDN'T WANT TO SHARE

In 1994, my assignment changed from the Russian Organized Crime Project to the Municipal Security Section, which we called MSS. It was headed by Inspector Dan Byrne. Byrne had been the boss of the criminal section in the Intelligence Division. He was pleased with the work I was doing, and in 1994, when Rudy Giuliani became Mayor, Byrne was appointed the head of MSS.

For those of you who are not familiar with the NYPD Intelligence Division, it was modeled after the US Secret Service (USSS). Part of the office worked in protection, performing escorts alongside the Secret Service and the US State Department protection team for heads of state and other dignitaries facing threats. Another part of the Division conducted Organized Crime Investigations, predominantly the Italian and Chinese gangs, and now the Russians. There was a third part of the Division that was secret, which handled deep-cover operatives embedded in radical organizations. The Detectives assigned here had new identities and no connection to the NYPD. Many of these men and women lived under deep cover for years, making incredible sacrifices.

Byrne was now responsible for protecting the elected officials, with both the uniformed section and the protective details reporting to him. One day, he called me to his office and asked if I had been working on anything that I couldn't put down for a few years. Reliving my prior experiences with the Chief, I decided not to try to be funny. I merely said no, but the thought crossed my mind that I was probably in trouble, and an indictment was coming down on me. That's the way cops think. It's like being called to the principal's office, but on steroids.

What he wanted was for me to be his assistant at MSS. For me, this was great. While I enjoyed the Russian Project, I was tired of criminal investigations and wanted to go into protection. That's what I wanted when I first went to Intel, but that got derailed.

I enjoyed the assignment and received training from the US Secret Service on physical security measures and threat assessments. We started a special unit in MSS called Protective Operations. Here, I was responsible for threat investigations and assessments, physical security, vehicles, and radio communications for the Mayor and the protectees covered under MSS. In addition, I was responsible for conducting and coordinating the site advance for the Mayor's attendance at a major event. All this experience leads me into the next round of chaos, the formation of the Office of Emergency Management under the direct control of Mayor Giuliani.

Rudy understood the need for a coordinated response to the City emergencies. The operation always involved multiple agencies responding to a crisis, and things never settled down fast enough. In 1996, he created the office as a Mayoral office; later, it became an agency with a Commissioner as its head. He appointed Jerome Hauer as his first Director in 1996.

The idea of emergency management in New York City was supposed to be simple: create one central agency to coordinate all others during a crisis. The problem was that in New York, every agency already considered itself the central agency.

The Office of Emergency Management was born out of chaos, and for a long time, it stayed there.

I was approached by Hauer one day at City Hall to see if I would help him find a suitable location for the Command Center he was planning to build. Using my training, experience, and common sense, I made a few recommendations. I learned quickly that he had a different idea about where it should be. If he could have put it under the Mayor's butt, he would have. Proximity to the Mayor was everything. If not directly under his feet, then it had to be within walking distance of him. Understand, this wasn't for quick access to the Mayor's command center; it was to ensure Hauer would never be that far away from the Mayor.

He also had grand ideas for what the command center would look like: large screens, open floor space, and no columns blocking views. The problem with this concept, albeit a good one, was that lower Manhattan in New York City didn't have many available locations with wide-open floor plans, and, according to the Army Corps of Engineers, we would be in a flood zone during a hurricane. It would be very embarrassing to have to close and evacuate the command center because of, let's say, flooding during a hurricane. The same reason we would all be at work was to respond to and manage the effects of a hurricane. Imagine doing that from a car on the side of the road? Or worse, having to borrow space from a different agency?

But location is everything, so he was able to find space on the 23rd floor of 7 World Trade Center. The Mayor asked me to go to OEM before the build-out. Given my involvement in security upgrades to the residences and offices, it made sense. Hauer was very open to the idea and may even have suggested it to the Mayor. He and I would work closely together for the next few years. What we developed was a love-hate relationship. Hauer was a fire buff; I was a cop. There was a natural rub. We fought like husband and wife privately. Publicly, we showed mutual respect.

We opened the new command center in 1996.

Once the lease for the new space at 7 World Trade Center was signed, the internal chaos began. We would have the entire 23rd floor. It had the open floor plan Hauer wanted, along with space for the offices and conference rooms we needed. It would house our Watch Command center, a press room capable of live feeds to the press trucks on the street, and a Mayoral office with a secure conference room. We weren't far off from how it was being designed. As a planning agency, one would have thought we were better at this than we were. Multiple revisions of the design were made. Many unintended consequences were never considered. In short, it looked very elaborate and pretty, but the functionality was greatly missing. Let me give you a few examples.

One issue with being twenty-three stories in the air was how the wind could affect the windows. There was concern that, in the event of a Category 5 hurricane, we possibly could lose the windows on the north side of the building. The air pressure would suck them right out according to the rules of physics. The countermeasure to this was to wrap the Emergency Operations Center and the Mayoral suite in reinforced ballistic walls. The walls were built with steel studs, 12 inches on center rather than the standard 16. They would be welded to the floor and ceiling structural steel. Over that were two layers of ¾ inch ballistic sheets, covered by two layers of ¾ inch sheet rock. The unintended consequence of this was the air within the space. The HVAC air-handling system needed to be large enough to serve the entire space. It wasn't. The only areas that had HVAC service were the Watch Command and Press room. If we ever had to hunker down and close the vents, the entire EOC staff would become groggy and fall asleep. Fortunately, we never had to hunker down.

Multiple press accounts questioned the rationale for building a bunker 23 stories above ground. I think the press enjoyed having fun poking at the office. In reality, it wasn't a bunker, but an office, but the facts didn't really matter. No matter where I go, for every speech or talk that I give, I am asked that question. My response is always the same: I wasn't the idiot who put it there; I was the idiot who had to defend it.

Once the buildout was complete, I would help write the City's plan for chemical and biological terrorism, bringing to the plans an Intelligence Operation. Having an intelligence aspect to what we were doing made perfect sense. I pitched the idea of creating an intelligence operation to both the Mayor and Hauer; each thought this was a great idea. It is important to remember that before 9/11, the NYPD did not have the global reach in intelligence it has today.

Today, in 2026, the NYPD's Intelligence Division is ranked among the world's best, rivalling that of small nations, but at the time, we made the best of what we had. The CIA was not going to share any active data openly with us. Forget the FBI. They wouldn't share a weather report, let alone threat information. As a leading agency in Emergency Management, we were approached by other jurisdictions and countries interested in our planning. I took advantage of the opportunity to establish relationships, including with foreign countries, to "share" our plans. The premise of "show me yours, and I'll show you mine" made perfect sense at the time.

As a result, I was made the Director of Security and Intelligence Operations for the Mayor's Office of Emergency Management.

At this point, we had a mandate so vague it could mean anything: "Coordinate citywide emergency response." Nobody said how, with whom, or under what authority. One of our coordinations was to allocate resources if and when an attack occurred.

At the time, the NYPD and FDNY were locked in a quiet but vicious turf war that went back decades. Both had their own command systems, radios, and egos. Cooperation wasn't just optional; it was offensive. During joint exercises to test plans to respond to issues like chemical and biological terrorism, each side kept adding more resources to the exercise to make sure they had more on scene than the other.

OEM was meant to break that pattern. In reality, it only exposed it.

Our first meetings looked less like planning sessions and more like divorce mediations. NYPD would sit on one side of the table, FDNY on the other, both with arms crossed, waiting for the other to blink. We'd start with simple topics: radio communication, resource sharing, and unified command. Within ten minutes, we'd be back to arguments about who got to talk first at press conferences. It took over a year to get an MOU signed that specified who was responsible for which events. The truth was, nobody wanted to share power, but everyone wanted to keep an eye on who might take it.

You would think getting them to agree might be simple, and it was simple until you got into the weeds. A fire was Fire's responsibility. Crime scenes were Police. But then, you get a chemical attack from a terrorist. Who is in charge? Fire says hazmat is in their purview. The Police say it was an intentional criminal act, and the scene is actually a crime scene. Everyone needed to stay out of the area.

One simple incident summed it up better than any chart or report could. I was in my office when I was told about a window washing rig that had collapsed downtown. One of the ropes holding the rig up breaks loose. The guy on the rig is in a safety harness, so he is not in danger of falling. The process is simple: go to the floor above, open the window, and pull him in.

So the NYPD Emergency Service Unit (our SWAT team) responds. They arrive at the apartment and ask the occupant if they can proceed with the rescue. Then comes the Fire Department. According to their belief, high-angle rescues are their responsibility. The Fire Lieutenant on the scene is greeted at the door by the NYPD and is denied access to the apartment. He takes exception to it. What happens next is still up for debate, as was the subsequent court case. What is not up for debate is the physical altercation that takes place in the apartment between the Fire Department personnel and the NYPD. All this while the poor bastard hanging off the scaffold is screaming at them to stop. Not to mention the person who let them into the apartment, who got to watch a WWF wrestling match on his couch instead of on TV.

We eventually implemented a few pilot programs and established policies for incidents involving multiple departments. It worked, sort of. But the moment the emergency ended, everyone returned to their silos. Communication between groups was something we practiced, not something we lived, at least not yet.

The irony was that OEM was supposed to centralize control, but it ended up exposing how decentralized the city really was. Even the smallest exercise revealed that coordination depended not on structure, but on personality. If you had the right mix of commanders on duty, things ran smoothly. If you didn't, you got chaos in stereo.

That realization became my first real leadership lesson inside OEM: structure doesn't save you, people do.

The chaos was cultural. OEM was seen as a threat to the authority of every other department. "Who the hell are you to tell us what to do?" became the unofficial greeting from the other agencies. We weren't trying to take control, we were trying to create order - but in New York, order looks a lot like politics.

When you're building an organization from scratch inside a system built on ego, the first thing you learn is humility. You can't demand cooperation; you have to earn it. Sometimes that means letting others take credit, even when you did the work. Sometimes it means smiling through meetings where everyone calls you useless until they need you.

By the end of that first year, we'd built something that almost looked like an agency. But what we really had was a fragile truce among rivals. Everyone wanted OEM to exist; nobody wanted it to lead.

The first real test for the Office of Emergency Management came before the paint on the walls was dry.

In July of 1996, TWA Flight 800 exploded off the coast of Long Island. Two hundred and thirty people were dead before the first responder arrived. Within an hour, the city was in a full-blown scramble. NYPD, FDNY, Port Authority, Coast Guard, FBI, NTSB, every agency imaginable flooded into the operation, each with its own command post, radios, and agenda. OEM was supposed to be the conductor of this orchestra, but we hadn't yet been given the baton.

The scene was chaos disguised as organization. Volunteers arrived unvetted, private boats joined search operations, and well-meaning community members started counseling family victims before the medical examiners even had names. Reporters swarmed the hotels where families were gathered, interviewing relatives as evidence was still being recovered from the ocean. There were no clear lines of control, only overlapping authority and emotional desperation.

That was when I realized OEM didn't just exist to coordinate, it existed to keep people from hurting each other while trying to help.

Later came another test. The city was planning a malathion-based mosquito-spraying campaign after an outbreak of West Nile virus. You'd think the operation would be straightforward: a few helicopters, some coordination, and public notice. Instead, it turned into another example of chaos.

At first, it came to us as a possible outbreak of Equine Encephalitis. Two elderly victims presented with the same symptoms of it. Both expired, and the Health Department was very concerned. To add to the chaos, we had received intelligence information that Saddam Hussein had been playing with using mosquitoes as a vector to deliver biological diseases. Could this be a terrorist attack? Something we were not prepared for.

Meetings are called quickly among us, the State Department, and the FBI. No one knows for sure, but it's possible. Further testing by the Health Department and CDC reveals it was West Nile. The countermeasure was to reduce the mosquito population. Malathion was the choice, but there was a rub. Earlier, we had published a book talking about how the average person can achieve chemical terrorism. Malathion is used in farming to control insects. If you bought it in large quantities, say a fifty-gallon drum of the type available to farmers, and processed it, you would end up with the same chemical composition as sarin gas. Boiled to a fifty percent reduction, you had a chemical agent that could kill. Now the decision was to overspray the city with Malathion. You see the problem here, right?

By the time the helicopters lifted off, the city had half the facts and none of the trust. Residents called 911, claiming they were being gassed. People thought they would be drenched if caught under the flight path. The reality was you wouldn't even notice.

OEM was caught in the middle, again. Our job wasn't to own the problem; it was to keep the problem from owning the city.

Then came the cyanide truck episode.

It was a simple call: a truck stolen from a transport company was carrying cyanide in barrels and a liquid identified as flammable flavoring liquid. Cyanide is apparently used to clean jewelry. The amount missing was enough to poison a city block.

We met with the Chief Medical Officer for New York City. The plan we came up with was simple. To counteract cyanide poisoning, you needed a special antidote. You only have a few minutes to initiate treatment before the person dies. Orders were sent to the NYPD and the FDNY; do not attempt to handle the barrels; wait for the antidote kits to arrive. We had about 50 kits in the office storeroom. The Chief Medical Officer for the City and I would split the kits and carry them in the trunks of our cars. If the barrels were found, we would both race to the scene.

A call comes in from the NYPD reporting that the barrels were found abandoned in the Bronx, next to a Little League field. I get the call and start responding to the scene. When I arrive, chaos is in full force.

Cops and firefighters - everyone wanted a piece of the action. FDNY and NYPD both set up perimeters. One declared it a rescue, the other a crime scene. Before long, they were shouting at each other across police tape.

When I arrived, both sides were furious. FDNY claimed ownership because there were chemicals involved. The NYPD claimed control because the vehicle was stolen, even though the truck was not there. Neither wanted to yield an inch. I got the Fire Chief and the Sergeant together. I asked whether there was any reason we were trying to rescue cyanide since the area was cordoned off and there was no indication it was off-gassing. Neither had a viable answer.

Using lessons learned from my time as a hostage negotiator, I orchestrated a "joint look down range." Both sides would send a couple of members, but none would share their radios. All I could do was calm egos long enough to get something done. The Fire Department sent two men, the Police sent two men, and the one guy from the Department of Environmental Protection went with them. All agreed the barrels were secured and not leaking. DEP called for Hazmat Transport, and the barrels were removed without further incident. With all the arguing and crying, the event ends with one man driving a large truck, smoking a cigarette. As if this wasn't just the biggest crisis in the City, he gets off the truck and asks, "What we got?" I give him the quick details, and he tosses the cigarette, goes to the barrels, and rolls them onto the truck tailgate. All by himself, no special hazmat gear, no special precautions.

When he drives back up to us, he gets out of the truck and lights up another cigarette. No one is saying anything, as we are all a little stunned. Looks at us like, what's the big deal?

He asks, "Anything else I can do for you guys?"

"No, I think we are good."

"OK, I'm going to lunch. Have a good day."

What was a crisis to us was a stop in his day. You would think those on the scene would have felt a little funny, or maybe embarrassed. But in true form, they didn't. Their ego was just too powerful.

I later learned an important lesson: when coordination exists without authority, government relies on process rather than leadership, and negotiation becomes the default rather than action. Without a formal hierarchical structure, we had to rely on trying to persuade individuals to work together. And that always came back to one thing. It always came back to personality. When the right commanders were on duty, the systems worked. When they weren't, it didn't.

OEM's biggest challenge wasn't logistics; it was pride. The city had spent decades rewarding individual heroism and punishing collaboration. Every department had its own mythology. NYPD saved the city from crime. FDNY saved it from fire. EMS saved it from death. But nobody wanted to save it from itself.

Fortunately, the City had ample resources to mitigate operational inefficiencies. With an army of over 60 thousand first responders at the time, even ego-driven mistakes were easy to overcome.

I started to recognize who the real leaders were. They weren't the loudest or highest-ranking people in the room. They were the ones willing to say, "What do you need?" instead of "Who's in charge?" Those were the people who kept the city running.

Still, progress came in inches, not miles. Every improvement had to be negotiated. When Motorola donated a device that enabled different radio bands to operate on the same frequency, allowing agencies to communicate directly, we thought the problem was solved. Instead, it became another turf war. Both the NYPD and the FDNY refused to participate. Neither agency was willing to provide a radio at the scene of an incident so that all agencies could communicate on a common command frequency. The irony and depth of the nonsense was that no agency would lose its radios. Each agency would still have its own radios to use on the scene. All we wanted was a common frequency for the incident commander to talk with other on-scene commanders from the different agencies. What we got was that the "children" didn't want to give up their "toys."

The device was never used.

From a leadership standpoint, these were some of the hardest lessons I've ever learned. You can't build a unified system on a foundation of fear. You can't coordinate people who see coordination as surrender. And you can't create leadership through mandate, it has to come from the willingness to let go of ego.

OEM forced the city to confront that reality. Every crisis became an X-ray of its leadership: who stepped up, who hid, who deflected, and who actually did the work.

By the late '90s, we had weathered chemical scares, disease outbreaks, and a dozen interagency standoffs. We had new procedures, new relationships, and a modest degree of credibility. But the truth was sobering: New York wasn't prepared because New York wasn't united. We were safe in spite of ourselves.

Looking back now, I realize OEM was a laboratory for leadership under chaos. It wasn't a story of technology or politics. It was about human behavior, how fear, pride, and inertia can grind down even the best ideas. We learned that structure doesn't automatically create leadership; communication does. And communication isn't a policy, it's a habit.

That was the irony at the heart of OEM's creation. We built an agency meant to control chaos, but what we really built was a mirror showing how much chaos already lived inside the system.

When I teach leadership today, I often return to that period, not because it was glamorous, but because it was honest. You don't lead in perfect conditions. You lead when people stop trusting each other, when communication breaks down, when politics replaces purpose. That's when leadership either shows up or disappears.

OEM taught me that crisis doesn't create character, it reveals it.

In January 2001, I decided to leave the civil service and move on to the next phase of my life. I approached the Mayor and told him privately of my plan. He was gracious and offered to help in any way he could. Many people working on the protective detail had made it their career and planned to stay with him after he left office in January 2002. I wanted to do it on my own. I had years of firsthand experience and a title that carried significant weight in the civilian world. I also had his endorsement, in case anyone asked for his opinion. The timing felt right for me.

Little did I know the worst terrorist attack on American soil was nine months away.

Leadership Principles

- Leadership in a city that refuses to cooperate isn't about power, it's about persuasion.

- The best leaders in chaos are translators: they turn the noise of competing agendas into a common language.

- Ego and authority are easy. Cooperation takes skill.

- Real leadership doesn't command the room; it connects it. If you can do that when everything around you is falling apart, you don't just manage chaos. You lead through it.

CHAPTER 7
TERRORISM, ALERTS, AND THE BUSINESS OF FEAR

I was home watching the morning news when 9/11 occurred. It was almost surreal, even for me, to sit and watch that happen. The original reports were that a small plane flew into the World Trade Center. I watched the video footage and immediately knew this was no small plane. The damn hole was just too big. We discussed a plane hitting the Trade Center, possibly a small Piper Cub, lost in the fog. Never was any thought given to a large commercial aircraft hitting it. From a terrorism perspective, the '93 bombing was almost understandable. Truck load of explosives, drive under the building, park it, and blow it up. But the thought of hijacking planes and hitting the buildings was never on the table. And the idea of hijacking multiple planes to hit all around the same time? How many of us can't coordinate a family get-together so everyone shows up on the same day? Forget about nearly the same time. And add the complexities of hijacking the planes. This was true planning and execution excellence.

In OEM, we did some really crazy planning for all types of terrorism events in the City. There were a few of us who would sit around a conference room table and say, "OK, let's screw the City today. What can we do to make that happen?" It was fun to let your mind run wild and think of all the ways a terrorist could attack. Things like a street festival where a bomb is detonated, and when the first responders come to the scene, the hotdog vendors' umbrellas release sarin gas.

There was clearly a purpose to what we were doing. If we consider how a terrorist could attack, however out-of-the-box, we can mitigate the effects. Questions can be thought of and answered before the event. Questions like, how many victims could there be? What do we need to pre-stage in the event of an attack? How much time would be required for the rescues? Where do we transport the victims? What capacity does each area hospital have to handle the flow? That was our planning process. Visualize what could be and plan for it. What we couldn't plan for was the effects of the fear.

It's hard to explain what fear does to a system until you've watched it consume one.

By the early 2000s, we had already endured years of bureaucratic infighting, broken communication, and turf wars that could fill a library. But when the words *terror threat* entered the public vocabulary, dysfunction became policy.

The idea of credible threat information was supposed to bring discipline and precision to how we assessed danger. Most people believe it means that the information we received was sufficient to support the act. What it really meant was the source was reliable, not that the information was accurate. In reality, it became the fuel for an entire economy of panic.

I first saw the cycle up close in the years after 9/11, though the groundwork had been laid long before. In 1993, when the first World Trade Center bombing ripped through the underground garage, most people thought of it as a fluke. When I moved from Intelligence to emergency management, we were still processing the lessons of that day. Our reports warned that future attacks would target the same symbolic assets: finance, transportation, and iconic structures. The economy of panic was born on that day in '93.

There was a rush to get new and emerging technologies into the hands of first responders. The amount of money that went down the proverbial rabbit hole was nearly incalculable. We called most of it "Vapor Ware" because it was about as effective as a vapor, no real effect, and lasted about as long. There was no standardization, no checks and balances, nothing but a pure rush to get solutions out to problems that weren't clearly identified.

Then 9/11 changed everything overnight. Suddenly, everyone wanted to be in the intelligence business. It even created a new "breed" of terrorism consultants. I call them the 9/12 experts. These were the people who went to the 9/11 sites and had their picture taken on the pile. With great admiration for themselves, they would tell you about their heroic actions of the day. Then they would sell a consulting service with all the credibility built into that picture.

If you're ever interested in reading a great book about the aftermath of 9/11 and what truly happened, I recommend William Langewiesche's *American Ground*. His firsthand account of the immediate aftermath of the towers' collapse offers detailed insight into what actually occurred. It's a story that was long overdue and needed telling.

I had the opportunity to meet him at a cocktail party thrown by John Oddermatt, the former Executive Officer and later the Director of OEM. I worked for John at OEM for the last few months before I left. He was a gentleman and made the last few months easier for me as I left the job.

During the party, I was introduced to Langewiesche, a moment that stands out in my memory. I knew he was a writer; he knew I was a former OEM member. What I didn't know then were his considerable accomplishments, both as a writer and in the immediate aftermath of 9/11.

Our conversation turned to September 11th, and I mentioned how important it would be if someone had the courage to write the real story, the events that didn't make the news, the parts that didn't fit the narrative where everyone was a hero. It was sensitive territory. The tragic loss of life and the exceptional stories of survival deserved their reverence. But there was a deeper, much darker side to 9/11 that also needed to be told. Langewiesche had the guts to write that book.

Before I continue, let me be clear: many who responded were pure of heart and wanted only to help. Many made the ultimate sacrifice, and those sacrifices continue today, with first responders still dying from injuries and exposure to toxins from working on the pile. That debt of gratitude can never be repaid.

But what I'm talking about goes beyond the opportunists who showed up just to get their picture taken and claim a career they didn't earn. Some came to steal from the remains, watches, and rings taken from body parts they found. Others took advantage of the chaos to loot stores and the scene itself.

A detective I worked with in the Protective Detail, Tibor Kerekes, who later became Deputy Police Commissioner of Administration under Bernie Kerik, explained this reality to me one day. We met at the new command center, and he was visibly upset. When I asked why, he told me he had just arrested someone for stealing a watch from the arm of a recovered body. I wish I could say events like this were rare, but the recovery period proved otherwise.

During our chance meeting, Langewiesche mentioned his book; he was the man who had the courage to write about these things. He was gracious enough to send me a copy, and it sits on the shelf behind my desk as a reminder.

The sacrifices and lifelong impact of that day will never be erased from our psyche. I've often said it was our generation's Pearl Harbor. The next generation will never share the same emotions and feelings we carry today. Unfortunately, these memories will pass on with us.

The events of 9/11 brought out deep, problematic planning issues for a City that thought it was invincible. In the City of 60,000 first responders, we felt we could never be overwhelmed in any situation. The arrogance and cockiness were pervasive. If there were a crisis anywhere domestically or abroad, the Mayor would be asked by FEMA to deploy the Urban Search and Rescue Team, USAR. In the event of a building collapse, hurricane, or earthquake, the Mayor would dispatch the USAR team to any State or Country in need of assistance. Wherever needed, they were eager to deploy.

The team consisted of members from the NYPD Emergency Service Unit, the Fire Department, and other City agencies, depending on the needs of the event they were responding to. I had the opportunity to deploy with them to Puerto Rico in response to Hurricane Hortense. In September 1996, Deputy Mayor Ninfa Segarra led the USAR team that traveled to the island to provide aid after Hurricane Hortense. Parts of the island were devastated, and the rebuilding would take time and money. Multiple deployments were made to Puerto Rico over the years, and the USAR teams were always ready to go. The teams' expertise was invaluable to the States or Countries they assisted.

With the cockiness and arrogance of having teams like that in our back pocket, we really felt that nothing would overwhelm us. We did not realize how sophomoric our attitude was. Our Police Department is ranked as a large army, with forty thousand sworn officers and thousands more in support staff. Our Harbor unit ranked as a small navy. Our aviation unit had sufficient flight operations to qualify as an air force, both with publicly known and unknown aircraft. Our Fire Department had over 12,000 personnel, with assets on land and water, and thousands more in civilian support roles. The Emergency Medical Services had thousands more to respond to any crisis. Not to mention the traffic agents and other large force City agencies that could respond in an emergency.

When planning and allocating resources, the question arises of when to call in the National Guard. It was always the question that got mocked. Answers such as "Why would we do that?" Or, why call them? Most of them work for the City; we would lose control over the people we need.

We always sent the teams to help; we never got to the point where we needed help. No, Sir, not us. 9/11 changed us forever that day. For once, we could not outsource or outmaneuver a crisis. This is the same argument we see today, with the Trump administration seeking to deploy the National Guard to address crime in major cities. The resentment among local administrations is similar to that in NYC before 9/11. Sometimes, you have to swallow your ego and ask for help.

The long-standing aftermath of 9/11 created much more chaos than any other event in the history of the City and possibly the country. As in the '93 bombing, there was a rush to deploy new technologies. This time, things were a little different: almost everyone asked how this could happen. What did we miss that should have told us it was coming? There was a rush for "intelligence information." Senate hearings were held to determine whether intelligence could have helped identify the risk and prevent it. "Intelligence" became the new buzzword.

Governors, mayors, corporations, you name it, they wanted their own security analysts, threat briefings, and color-coded charts. Information that had once been locked in a vault now poured out like a firehose, but with no filter. Everyone was sharing everything, except the parts that mattered. Data, by itself, is not intelligence. How it is analyzed makes it worthwhile intelligence.

That's when Washington introduced the Homeland Security Advisory System (HSAS) in

2002, by the Bush administration following the 9/11 attacks. The system used five colors (Green, Blue, Yellow, Orange, Red) to indicate threat levels and was replaced by the National Terrorism Advisory System in April 2011. The meanings of each color are Green (Low), Blue (Guarded), Yellow (Elevated), Orange (High), and Red (Severe).

It sounded scientific, like a weather forecast for terror. But it wasn't based on science. It was based on politics, fear, and plausible deniability. Some barely used it. New York City was perpetually on "Orange" or high alert.

We joked that "yellow" meant we have no idea, "orange" meant someone's covering their ass, and "red" meant someone's already on TV.

In theory, each level corresponded to specific countermeasures. In practice, it triggered a single reaction across the board: overtime. Every city would flood the streets with a visible presence: police in tactical gear, officers with long rifles in train stations, checkpoints at bridges, and canine units sniffing every moving thing. It looked like readiness. It was really theater.

A few months after one of those national "orange alert" weeks, I got a call about a "credible threat" that summed up everything wrong with how we were operating.

A truck driver in Florida had overheard two men in a diner talking about "blowing up the bridge." He didn't know who they were, missed the context, and didn't hear a specific location. But he was considered a credible source; he'd helped police before. That single detail changed everything. His reputation became credibility, not the information.

Within hours, alerts went out to state agencies across the East Coast. Local police sealed off highways, Homeland Security raised the advisory level, and television anchors stood on bridges giving live updates about "imminent threats." The FBI spent days chasing ghosts through half a dozen states.

Ultimately, it was two men arguing over coffee about terrorism: no plot, no bomb, no bridge. Just talk.

But by then the damage was done. The headlines had already written the story, and the system had done what it always did: overreact first, verify later.

That's the dangerous equation fear creates, once the public hears the word terror, you can't take it back. You can't walk a city off the ledge. It's easier to mobilize an army than to convince people they're safe.

The public didn't know that credible threat information didn't mean credible threat. It meant the source was credible. That's how you get an entire nation to move resources based on gossip.

I watched the transformation happen in real time. Inside briefings, analysts would present vague intelligence, then add the unspoken truth: "We can't ignore it, because if we do and something happens, we're done." That was the primary motivator: fear of accountability.

Worry had replaced leadership.

The term *credible threat* was never about accuracy; it was about liability. You couldn't be blamed for overreacting, only for underreacting. The political calculus was simple: if nothing happened, you were careful. If something did, you could say you warned everyone.

The cost of that logic was staggering. Every elevation in alert level costs millions in overtime, logistics, equipment, fuel, manpower. We were burning through budgets faster than the enemy could plan. And the irony was that the attacks we feared most weren't coming. We were outspending our adversaries by a thousand to one and still losing the psychological war.

Bin Laden understood that better than anyone. After 9/11, he didn't have to attack again. All he had to do was talk. Every time he released a tape or issued a statement, the markets dipped, airports froze, and government officials called emergency meetings. He was fighting a war of perception, and we were paying for it with taxpayer money and national anxiety. We were too stupid to realize the attack was the threat.

A notable example was in the summer of 2004, when the Republican National Convention was held in New York at Madison Square Garden. The City had deployed tens of thousands of officers, sealed entire streets, and allocated more than $60 million in security for a single week. Why? Because Bin Laden had released a threat. We jumped high, exactly as he expected.

Our new American motto should have become, *"In fear we trust."*

The business of fear had become self-sustaining. The media needed threats to fill airtime. Politicians needed to look decisive. Security vendors needed to sell hardware. Everyone was profiting from anxiety, and no one was measuring results. You couldn't. One of the most difficult things to do is to prove a negative. If you plan and nothing happens, was it because of the planning, or because nothing was going to happen? The more nothing happened, the more people profited by it.

The threats and overreactions left agencies fatigued. Officers were on 16-hour shifts in response to threats that never materialized. Executives were terrified of being the one who "missed the signal." Entire units were devoted to managing the optics of readiness. We were living in a feedback loop in which perception dictated policy, and policy reinforced fear.

That was when I began using a rule I learned in Threat Management School and still apply in every crisis briefing: "Worry is not a tactic." That single sentence was delivered in a book written by Gavin De Becker called "The Gift of Fear." In it, he talks about the fear stalking victims feel and how they respond to it. That line is often applied today. When you worry about an issue or situation, you think you are actively working on it. All you are doing is wrapping yourself around the axle and getting nowhere to solve the problem.

You'd be amazed at how many leaders confuse activity with strategy. They think motion equals progress, noise equals preparedness. Most of what passed for counterterrorism in those years was choreography, designed to show the public that someone was in charge, even when no one really was. Let's deploy armed police officers with assault rifles to protect against a threat that was six months old. It really was that pathetic.

The truth is that fear is profitable. It moves budgets, elections, and ratings. The news doesn't sell calm; it sells crisis. Politicians don't win votes by saying "we're probably fine." The easiest way to sound decisive is to act alarmed.

I see leaders fall into that trap repeatedly. The moment a threat hits their desk, they'd scramble to hold press conferences, raise alerts, and issue sound bites like "out of an abundance of caution." They believed that doing *something*, even if it made no sense, was better than being accused of doing nothing.

That's not leadership. That's fear management.

As many authors have said before, authentic leadership demands the courage to say no when everyone around you is screaming, "Do something." It's not glamorous, and it rarely gets applause. But it's the only way to maintain credibility over time. Once you start chasing every rumor, you lose the ability to tell people when a threat actually matters. A real-life example, not related to terrorism, but still a perfect example of overreaction and warnings: the weather forecasts. How many times are we told the end is near, historic flooding and feet of snow are on the way, only to see the sunshine or have a minor sprinkle from above? If we ever need a good example of information fatigue, it is in the weather forecasts. Accuracy is not a prerequisite. It would be interesting to study how many lives were lost due to warnings being ignored, given the too-frequent, unnecessary evacuation notices, but I digress.

I began to see a clear divide between leaders who understood risk and those who understood only politics. The first group asked, "What is the probability and what are the consequences?" The second group asked, "What will the headline be if I'm wrong?" The second group always won.

There is a quote attributed to Danny Miranda, *"You can't outrun fear by moving faster. You beat it by thinking slower."* This concept, I later discovered, became the foundation of my subsequent training, the mindset that would eventually evolve into the STOP Technique, which I will cover later in this book. Because at its core, fear is a speed problem. The faster you react, the less you think. The less you think, the more you repeat mistakes.

The post-9/11 era was full of speed. Everyone wanted instant answers, instant reassurance, instant response. The faster the world demanded action, the less space there was for reason.

It wasn't just governments. Corporations followed the same model. Every time there was a global incident, a bombing, a cyberattack, a disease outbreak, executives would send out statements within minutes. Most were meaningless. They were written for optics, not accuracy. Fear had become part of corporate branding.

Over time, I learned to distinguish between resilient and performative organizations. The resilient ones asked questions before they acted. The performative ones acted to avoid being questioned.

One leadership lesson is that calm is not inaction. Calm is control. It's the refusal to let your emotions dictate the direction you take. In crisis management, that's the difference between surviving and collapsing. During my years on the NYPD Hostage Negotiation Team, we were trained to slow things down in a crisis. Don't let the adrenaline rush push you into actions that could provide disastrous outcomes. At first, it seems counterintuitive, but the tactic works. When SWAT teams planned "dynamic entries," we wanted to talk. That caused friction at times, but over time, they came to recognize its effectiveness.

Every day brings a new alert, a new "credible report," a new request from the media. The question the media always asks me is: "Is this real?"

How do I respond without causing chaos?

Over the years, in my many news media appearances, I know the media wanted "inside information." What was I hearing? What can I tell the public about the current threats?

The people you see on the news media have about as much information as you do. Sure, we hear rumors and can sometimes translate what I call "Fed Speak," those cryptic public relations memos and notices that come out all too often. But in reality, if a credible threat did exist, it would be under active investigation by law enforcement. There is no way they would be telegraphing the information about an active case. I always try not to be the guy on TV playing "Chicken Little" and saying the sky is falling. Those pundits who do are trying to capture lightning in a bottle. If they are ever right, they appear to be the most insightful person in the world. When they are wrong, no one remembers what they said. The news cycle is just too fast to go back and catch them, let alone hold them accountable. Besides, it makes for great TV.

For those like me on TV, it's a balancing act: making people aware without making them fearful.

I'd go on air and tell people the same thing I told my own staff: *Stay alert, not afraid.*

The first time I said it, a producer asked me to repeat it on air because they said it sounded "too reasonable for TV." That was the world we were living in; reason had become a novelty.

As we will see next, reason may be a novelty, but not as novel as common sense. As the saying goes, common sense is not as common as it once was.

....

Leadership Principles

- Every false alarm, every overreaction, every headline chasing "credible information" teaches the same lesson: credibility and truth are not the same thing.

- When everyone else is running, the leader's job isn't to run faster, it's to slow the room down.

CHAPTER 8
YOU CANNOT MAKE THIS STUFF UP: THE AX HANDLE AND THE BOAT

After 9/11, security became like a national religion.

The Transportation Security Administration (TSA) acted as its clergy. Every airport in America transformed into a cathedral of compliance. Shoes off, belts off, laptops out, liquids bagged, bottles under three ounces, and patience under one minute. Somewhere between gate check and body scan, the country convinced itself that inconvenience meant safety.

On paper, TSA was created to protect travelers. In practice, it became a monument to inconsistent logic. Every traveler has a story. Some are mildly annoying; others are unbelievable. This one is somewhat in the middle, and I assure you, it's true. It's too stupid not to be.

It happened a few weeks after flights resumed following 9/11. A friend of mine, a senior pilot for a major international airline, was flying out of New York. He was in full uniform, credentials around his neck, hat under his arm, the picture of authority. He was going to be the Pilot in Command of this flight. He'd flown through war zones, across oceans, through storms. He'd logged more hours in the cockpit than most TSA officers had spent on the job. When he reached the gate, TSA was conducting "secondary screenings," a new layer of protection intended to reassure passengers. A young agent, by all appearances earnest, polite, and new, stopped him for inspection. He cooperated without complaint. His attitude was that the plane is going nowhere without me, so what the hell, let's do this. He'd seen enough chaos to know resistance was pointless. She opened his carry-on and began to search. Inside, she found a small shaving kit. She unzipped it, looked inside, and froze. "Sir," she said solemnly, "I'm going to have to confiscate these scissors." He looked down. In her hand was a tiny pair of cuticle scissors, thin, delicate, the kind you could barely trim a string with. "You're joking," he said, smiling. "No, sir. These can be used as a weapon." He stared at her for a moment, trying to decide if it was a test.

"A weapon?" he asked.

"Yes, sir. These could be held against the pilot's throat and used to hijack the plane."

He blinked.

"Madam, you do realize I am the pilot of this plane, right?"

She didn't laugh. Rules were rules. The scissors were placed in a confiscation bin filled with nail clippers, tweezers, and small scissors belonging to other dangerous travelers. He shrugged and boarded the plane. As he sat in the cockpit preparing for takeoff, he glanced over his left shoulder, and there it was. Mounted to the wall behind him was a full-sized, steel-bladed hand ax. It was part of the emergency equipment on every commercial aircraft, designed to break through doors or windows in a crash. The absurdity was impossible to ignore. The same pilot who couldn't carry a tiny pair of scissors past security now sat next to an actual ax. Rules had replaced reasoning.

The front lines of national defense were now manned by people trained to enforce regulations without understanding them. The government had created a system that valued compliance over comprehension.

In fairness, TSA agents weren't the villains. They are soldiers in a system that punishes critical thinking. Following policy kept you safe; using judgment could get you fired. That's how fear-driven systems sustain themselves, by removing discretion.

During those early post-9/11 years, I saw that same logic infect every level of public safety. Decisions were made not for effectiveness, but for appearance. A rule wasn't judged by whether it worked; it was judged by whether it looked tough.

There was an old saying among cops: "If it makes sense, it's probably against policy." TSA turned that into a rule.

One month, they banned box cutters, which made sense. Next, they confiscated gel inserts from shoes because someone tried to hide explosives inside his sneakers. When passengers began bringing snow globes as gifts, TSA banned them as well, citing "liquid." It didn't matter that they posed less of a threat than a soda can. The rule existed, so it needed to be enforced.

That's how bureaucracy works: once you make a rule, you must defend it. It becomes sacred. Challenging it means challenging the people who created it, and no government worker has ever been promoted for admitting that a rule was foolish.

The result is a culture of ritual. Passengers take off shoes, agents scan bags, alarms beep, and the illusion of control continues like clockwork. It doesn't matter if the system detects anything. What matters is that it appears to be able to.

That lesson stuck with me. I saw the same pattern in OEM and NYPD Intelligence: when organizations stop trusting their people to think, they start creating systems to do it for them. Those systems often become more important than the mission itself.

That's how you end up with a pilot who's stripped of scissors and handed an ax.

The story of the scissors and the hand ax spread through the aviation community like folklore. Pilots shared it in break rooms, I'm sure passengers recounted it in bars, and every security professional I knew added their own twist to emphasize the same point: when policy loses its context, common sense dies first. In today's world, common sense is not so common anymore.

I began collecting similar stories, not because they were funny, but because they served as warnings. They showed how quickly an organization built on fear can slip into absurdity. Once rules become more important than reasoning, failure isn't just possible, it's inevitable.

There have been many stories, more than I can cover in a single book. But there are the winners, the ones that you say to yourself, you can't make this shit up!

Within the first week after 9/11, I was contacted by the Department of Justice representative I had been working for as a "Technical Assistance Provider." He asked if I could head into the City and see what, if anything, they may need that we could help with. I was eager to go and try to be helpful. In those days after 9/11, I was itching to get back. I was like the old Dalmatian dog in the firehouse, the bell rang, and I still wanted to go. But I knew that showing up unannounced would only add to the confusion, so I waited for a call that finally came.

I knew that OEM had been working out of the Police Academy since 9/11. The command center we built was destroyed that day. It was the last building to fall. I headed in and spoke with John Odermatt, who was now in charge. I asked what, if anything, I could do to help. He told me that Pier 52 on the west side of Manhattan would be the new temporary command center for the City. He had no one available to set it up. Would I be able to help with that? My response was a quick yes, and I was off to complete it.

When I got to the pier, I realized things were much worse than I expected. There were no resources available. I expected the NYPD would have a detail of cops there to protect it. There were none. I called the Operations desk at Police Headquarters and spoke to a friend. He told me the Department had no one. I was going to be on my own, use what I could muster. The risks at this point were high; we didn't know if planes would continue to hit us, if the coordinated attack would continue with localized explosives. Here we were, with our ass sticking into the Hudson River, the new nerve center of the City, and we had no security at all. Well, that's not totally accurate. I did have a volunteer show up that day with a police dog. You would think I would be appreciative, but let me explain. He was a retired Police Lieutenant from a small Connecticut Town. He was about 80 years old, and the dog was a toothless police dog. Somehow, the saying of making lemonade from lemons just didn't fit. This was going to be more complicated than I thought.

The next few days were a crush of equipment deliveries, people trying to set up computers, and City leadership coming and going. Slowly, we started to get it together. The NYPD Harbor teams, along with the Coast Guard, kept watch from the water. They would patrol past every once in a while. I was concerned about the underwater section of the pier; it would be easy for scuba divers to place explosives under the dock and blow us up. At this point, nothing was off the table regarding the risks we might face. At night, a couple of us would stand out on the pier, facing the water. We would look for anything suspicious floating by. If we saw something, we would shine a heavy-duty handheld spotlight on it and try to follow it. Either the Coast Guard or the NYPD Harbor teams would go to the location where we were shining the light and attempt to identify it. That was if the timing was right and they were in the area. Otherwise, we stood there wondering what was coming next.

A few days into the setup, I'm asked to meet a Lieutenant from Naval Intelligence at the pier entrance. The Lieutenant is a woman in her full uniform, smartly dressed, all pressed, and with an air of confidence and professionalism. She introduces herself and explains that she is doing an advance for the US Comfort, which will be docked alongside our pier. The USS Comfort is a hospital ship capable of treating injured soldiers in combat. It can also accommodate large groups, providing food, shelter, and sleeping accommodations. The thought process was to have it docked by us and transport the workers from the World Trade Center site, known as the "pile," to the ship by bus. The groups would rotate every 12 hours, allowing them to eat, wash up, change clothes, and get much-needed sleep.

I explained to her that putting the boat there was a poor choice. For starters, it had a big red X on top. Actually, it was a red cross, but as far as I was concerned, it looked like a big red X. X marks the spot, as the saying goes. Let's give the attackers a slight advantage by making it easy for them to spot the target.

She looks at me and says, "Sir, I must inform you that it is a ship, and not a boat."

I shake my head. With everything going on, this one wants to have a semantic conversation.

"Lieutenant, we have no security here. If the decision is made to put it here, then can you provide security for the dock?"

She shakes her head and says, "No."

OK, I'll bite, "Why?"

She stands slightly more erect, as if that was even possible, and says, "It's the law, Posse Comitatus. We are precluded by that law from providing police operations to non-military assets."

I shake my head, trying to make room for that to fit in.

"Lieutenant, you do understand that we are at significant risk here. The possibility of further attacks has not been ruled out. Tying your boat to my dock, which has no security, makes no sense. Do you understand that?"

Her reply should have indicated where this conversation was going.

"Sir, I need to remind you that it is a ship and not a boat."

"Ok, ok, but you will have security here with it, correct?"

"That is correct, but only for the ship and not the dock."

"Can you explain the difference to me? You will have security, but not for the dock it's tied to. How does that make any sense?"

Her frustration is becoming more evident.

"Sir, I explained that to you, Posse Comitatus."

"So security for the boat and not for the dock, I can't wait to see how that works out."

"Sir, please, it is a ship and not a boat."

"Lieutenant, just understand that I am advising you that when my pier gets blown up, your fucking boat is going to sink! Have a nice day!"

I walked away shaking my head, fearing that if this was Naval Intelligence, we as a country were in serious trouble.

After regaining my composure, I knew I still needed some help. I decided to call a friend I knew in Naval Intelligence to see if he had any suggestions. It took him a while to stop laughing and breathe again. When he finally settled down, he said to stand by; he would call me back. In twenty minutes, he called and told me there were a couple of vans full of Marines heading my way. Sure enough, 20 minutes later, they pulled up.

A sharply dressed Captain got out of the front passenger seat of the first van and introduced himself.

"Sir, we have been sent here to set up security for the USS Comfort."

And with a smirk on his face, "with your permission, we would like to be able to provide security for the dock so that if something bad does happen, our 'fucking boat' won't sink."

I had to laugh. It was the first time that week that there was something to laugh about.

The scissors and the ship were two sides of the same coin; rules applied without understanding context. In both cases, rigid policy replaced judgment. TSA was protecting against cuticle scissors while ignoring the ax. The Navy was protecting jurisdictional boundaries while ignoring the threat.

In the years after 9/11, I worked with numerous agencies and corporate security teams to rebuild their posture. Each of them had adopted a version of the same approach: more rules, more steps, more checklists. Each new policy was another patch meant to cover a liability, but nobody stopped to ask whether the patches actually fit.

I remember sitting in on a meeting with a corporate security director who proudly announced that his company had implemented "zero discretion" protocols. Every guard was to follow the manual word for word, no exceptions, no judgment calls, no thinking. He feared that he had very little, if any, confidence in the guards. The thought rushed back to times when I would create a checklist for something. When using it for the first time, after the first or second line, what I had didn't fit. I asked him how he planned to handle a situation that didn't fit the checklist.

He smiled and said, "We'll update the manual."

That was the mindset we faced. The sense of having control had overshadowed the goal of developing competence.

That's what TSA embodies today. It isn't evil. It's scared. The system is terrified of another failure, so it trades judgment for process. Today, it created a world where confiscating nail clippers made more sense than questioning why.

When you remove discretion from the field, you remove leadership from the equation. A good policy can guide a decision, but it can't replace the decision maker. Leadership demands understanding the intent behind the rule, not just the wording. Without that understanding, you're left with mechanical obedience. And mechanical obedience can't adapt to chaos. Many Police Departments have rule books and procedures. In the NYPD, it is called the Patrol Guide. It is the bible you live by, but it is also a "guide."

Jeffrey Pfeffer, in his book *Leadership BS: Fixing Workplaces and Careers One Truth at a Time*, offers a compelling analogy for what was happening. He said, "In leadership, that trade-off is fatal. Fear breeds procedure; procedure breeds stagnation. Over time, the organization becomes so rigid that its people stop learning. They follow orders because it's safe, not because it's right."

I saw that culture of fear migrate from government into corporate America. After every major incident, an active shooter, a cyberattack, or a public scandal, companies panic and respond with blanket policies. HR rolls out new training modules. Legal adds disclaimers. The executives are proud to declare that new rules and procedures are in place to correct the mistakes that occurred. But what they rarely say is: "Lesson learned, I know what happened, but never really understand the why." If they do go there, they rush to a decision too quickly. Later in this book, I will describe a process that slows down thinking and prevents a rush to judgment.

At PCC Secure, I built our training philosophy around that distinction. We teach the *why*, not just the *what*. If an officer understands *why* a policy exists, they can adapt it intelligently. If they only know *what* to do, they freeze the moment something doesn't match the manual.

Every class we teach comes back to that same idea: leadership is not compliance. It's comprehension.

That's the difference between a guard who confiscates scissors and one who recognizes the ax behind the seat.

The more profound lesson is that organizations must decide whether they value risk reduction or understanding more. The first minimizes exposure; the second builds resilience. Bureaucracies always pick the first because it's quantifiable. What is the reduction in insurance premiums? What is the cost to the brand if something happens? What are the legal costs to defend? These are all quantifiable; asset management can create a spreadsheet and present the hard numbers. Leaders choose the second because it's sustainable. You can make the case that understanding has a perceived value that plays out over the long run, but it is virtually impossible to show a calculable number.

What I am not saying is that you need to disregard the risk or place less importance on it. Some might equate what I am saying to the "what comes first, the chicken or the egg?" This is not the case. In my opinion, understanding the reasons behind the risks is more important than identifying them at first. There have been countless times when I have conducted a security system audit and found that the systems in place have capabilities far beyond what was needed. The amount of money spent on bells and whistles that never get used, never get practiced with, or, in the worst cases, are totally forgotten about, yet are continually paid for year after year. By understanding the risks, you can make an informed decision about which processes or countermeasures to implement. When the risks are identified too early without understanding the why, it can lead to chaos.

In security work, there's a dangerous comfort in rules. They feel safe. They promise certainty in a world that doesn't offer it. But safety isn't the absence of risk, it's the presence of awareness. Real safety comes from trust and training, not from confiscation bins. Training costs money, and the return on investment, ROI, is not easily determined.

The battles between the asset management department and the security departments are as intense as those between the security and IT departments. For asset management, life is a series of spreadsheets. What do the numbers say? How does this fit into a budget? Is it really worth the money? Provide a cost-benefit analysis to determine whether this is worth it. How many times have we heard this conversation?

The frustration here is that you are being asked to provide an answer to prove the negative. That is almost, if not totally, impossible. If a security countermeasure is put in place and nothing happens, did it really prevent the event from occurring? You will never know for sure.

At the onset of COVID, clients asked me to suggest ways to reduce security staffing and cut budgets. All understandable at the time. Buildings were operating at almost no occupancy. When COVID concerns eased and people began returning to work, I recommended a gradual return to the original staffing levels.

The response was, "Do we really need all those people? Nothing happened."

From an asset management perspective, "What are we paying for if nothing happens? "Show me a need, and I can adjust the budget," was the response, always.

I had to develop a counterargument to this argument. I decided to take a page from their own playbook and use a spreadsheet as the defensive weapon. I created a metric for the number of people a security team reviews each year. It was a count of the number of people who entered a facility or commercial real estate property. This is how the sheet breaks down.

The property has approximately 5,000 tenants. That's 5,000 people arriving in the morning. That means 5,000 people leaving at night. We knew from the turnstile reports that about 30% of the people went to lunch. They leave and return, resulting in two additional views. When you add up the total number of people per day, you get 10,600 people walking past security. That was just the occupants. We are now adding 2,000 visitors per day. That's a total of 4,000 people to watch. We are up to 14,600 people coming and going in front of them daily, Monday through Friday. Multiply that by 5 days per week and 52 weeks per year. The numbers are staggering: 73,000 a week, not counting weekends. Multiply that by 50 weeks per year, accounting for holidays, and you have a total of 3,650,000 people they must observe. I didn't count packages or deliveries. Two to three guards perform all this at $18 per hour. With nearly 4 million people coming and going, is it not safe to say something was prevented?

As the years go on, I find myself less interested in the policies and more interested in the people who enforce them. The best front-line personnel, whether cops, guards, TSA agents, or National Intelligence agencies, were the ones who quietly applied logic even when the rules didn't fit. They treated the manual as a guide, not a gospel. These people keep systems functional, even when leadership didn't deserve it.

And that's what *Leading Through Chaos* is really about. Every system breaks down under pressure. Every rulebook eventually meets a situation it can't cover. When that happens, survival depends not on compliance, but on clarity. You can't train people to memorize their way out of chaos; you have to train them to think.

That's what the TSA and Naval Intelligence stories teach, whether you're managing an airport, a company, or a city: policy without understanding is just noise. The leader's job is to turn that noise into knowledge.

Because when the world starts confiscating scissors and handing out axes, someone has to be the one to say, "This makes no sense."

Another major issue, to "you can't make this stuff up", comes from leaders who push the envelope and do things to stretch the limits of security operations. They fail to inform security of events or parties with hundreds of people and say, "It's going to be OK." After you voice concerns, they look at you and say, "You are worrying about nothing." The event occurs, and nothing bad happens. After the event, they look at you and say, "See, I told you so."

Were they right or were they lucky? You will never know. The politics of the situation come into play. I always say that 85% of my job is to deal with politics. Very little of the consulting comes from the actual security management. Next, I will go in-depth on the politics of most situations and how they drive outcomes.

. . . .

Leadership Principles

- Leadership requires dialogue. The next time you write a policy or enforce one, ask yourself if you understand its purpose, or if you're repeating someone else's fear.

- Leaders think through the "why." Followers hide behind the "what."

- If you want your team to think on their feet, permit them to question the rulebook. That's where real security and authentic leadership begin.

CHAPTER 9
POLITICS, EGO, AND THE FIRST TWENTY-FOUR HOURS.

Every disaster has two beginnings: the event itself and the first press conference about it.

Those of us who work in crisis management know that the second one often does more damage than the first.

In the hours after any significant incident, the facts are scarce, emotions are high, and cameras are already rolling. It's in that window, before facts replace rumors, that leadership either stabilizes the system or sets it on fire. And far too often, the people behind the podium are the last ones qualified to speak.

During my years with the Office of Emergency Management, I saw more "first twenty-four hours" than I can count. Fires, explosions, chemical scares, blackouts, and near-misses each brought their own chaos. At the Federal

Level, and even at the international level, what never changes is how quickly politics takes over operations.

Leaders want to look decisive. The responders want to get the job done. The media wants a headline. Somewhere in the middle sits' reality, gasping for air.

The anatomy of a political response is always this: optics first, accuracy later.

It wasn't just local politics either. The same pattern repeated at every level of government and corporate America. After 9/11, there was an unspoken competition among agencies to "own" the narrative of preparedness. Everyone wanted to look like the hero in the next briefing. And when ego meets fear, truth becomes a casualty.

The problem is that modern politics treats uncertainty like weakness. But in real crisis work, uncertainty is honesty. You can't lead without admitting what you don't know.

That's why the first twenty-four hours after any incident are so dangerous. The need to sound in control often overrides the need to *be* in control. Leaders issue statements before facts exist. They make promises before options are clear. They give orders before experts finish speaking.

And those early decisions, made for television, can haunt operations for days.

The best example of this was a person we all remember as "Baghdad Bob" or "Comical Ali."

Mohammed Saeed al-Sahhaf, famously nicknamed "Baghdad Bob" or "Comical Ali" by Western media, became an unlikely source of comedy during the tense days of the 2003 Gulf War invasion. As Iraq's Minister of Information, al-Sahhaf held daily press briefings with dramatic flair, boldly claiming Iraqi dominance even as coalition forces steadily advanced toward Baghdad. His statements, filled with apparent bravado, created a false sense of invincibility that was clearly contradicted by the reality on the ground. Despite clear evidence of coalition tanks entering the city, Baghdad Bob strongly insisted that no such presence existed. His denials were not subtle diplomatic maneuvers, but flamboyant declarations shouted into the cameras, creating an almost surreal effect. Far from maintaining a stoic front, he seemed caught up in a ridiculous act, trying to uphold a facade of strength that drew both confusion and amusement worldwide. Al-Sahhaf's performance was particularly humorous because of his consistent use of exaggerated language and colorful insults aimed at the U.S. His passionate outbursts, filled with bravado and outlandish claims of Iraqi victories, turned him into a kind of propaganda caricature. Though his speeches aimed to boost confidence among Iraqi supporters, they unintentionally revealed outright dishonesty, exposing a man desperately trying to lift morale amid apparent defeat. Ultimately, "Baghdad Bob" became a symbol not only of Saddam Hussein's regime but also of how far propaganda can go during a crisis. His dramatic claims, delivered with unwavering confidence despite apparent contradictions, made him an unintentional yet memorable comic figure in the grim reality of war.

That's the paradox of modern leadership: you can correct an action you did, but you can't correct a sound bite.

Over the years, I learned to anticipate this. Every time a crisis breaks, I try to think of two decision trees, one for the facts and one for the politics. The first concerns reality; the second, perception. The goal is to keep them from destroying each other. Perception should never become reality, but sometimes, when you combine it with ego, the result is unbelievably ridiculous. I learned this on two occasions while at the Pier during the 9/11 response.

One afternoon, a good friend, Sean Waters, approached me to tell me something he didn't believe himself. Sean worked for FEMA and was positioned on the Pier next to ours. We had worked together in OEM, and he had moved on to FEMA's planning and response section. He was short, stocky, had a great sense of dry humor, and didn't like the politics and ego of political hacks. When it came to patience for stuff like this, he made me look like a saint.

"I have someone who wants to talk to you from Washington."

I was curious, thinking maybe something I said to the Lieutenant from Naval Intelligence was getting around to bite me in the ass.

"What's up?"

"There is a guy from FEMA headquarters here who wants to come over and measure the mayor's desk."

I wasn't totally sure whether he was having a good laugh or was serious. Turns out he was serious.

"Apparently, the Director of FEMA is visiting and wants a desk next to the Mayor.

The Director at the time, during the September 11, 2001, terrorist attacks, was Joseph Allbaugh, appointed by President George W. Bush, responsible for leading the agency's response to the World Trade Center and Pentagon attacks. It seemed like he thought he needed to be working side by side with the Mayor, so a flunky was sent over to measure the mayor's desk.

Sean tried to explain to him that there were a couple of issues for this flunky to deal with. First, the guy he was bringing him over to meet, me, had no sense of humor at that time. Second, the Mayor had no desk, nothing to measure.

The flunky insisted on coming over to meet with me. Sean couldn't wait to see what was about to happen. Gleefully, Sean escorted the gentleman over to introduce him to me.

I shook hands with the guy and asked what was going on.

"What can I help with?" I asked him.

He tells me the same story he gave Sean. He is instructed to see the Mayor's office on the Pier and measure the Mayor's desk.

I shake my head again to try to clear my thoughts, and ask why?

His response was quick and to the point.

"Director Allbaugh will arrive this afternoon, and we need a desk for him in the Mayor's office. I need to measure it because the desk cannot be smaller than the Mayor's, but it cannot be larger either. You understand, don't you?"

"Are you fucking kidding me?'

"No, sir, these are my orders."

I can't help but call him "Foggy."

"Look, Foggy, first up, the Mayor doesn't have a desk. He is working off a 4X8 sheet of plywood on two wooden horses. Second, I'm not setting anything up for the Director without first speaking with the Mayor. I am not sure I want to bring this up with him now, given everything going on."

I start to walk away to try to dismiss him, but I turn back.

"This is fucking absurd. We are in real trouble if the Director of FEMA is thinking about this now."

"Foggy" is unfazed by my rebuttal. He is duty-bound, as I would often say of people like this. What comes next deserves a medal, one for him and one for me.

"Sir, you need to understand that I am under direct orders from the President of the United States to conduct this."

I had to give the kid credit; in the grip of failure, he comes up with some exquisite bullshit. He deserved a medal for his try.

"Look, Foggy, if that's true, and I severely doubt that it is, go back and tell George that I won't do it. If he has a problem with it, he should call me."

I should have gotten a medal for not shooting the incompetent bastard and dumping him in the river.

The second incident occurred the same day as the FEMA fiasco. I reached out to Sean to tell him I'd seen his example of stupidity and could raise him one. He thought he had me beat, but in the end, I won. I swear this story is true, too. This did not come from hearsay but from a first-person account, me.

I'm standing on the Pier, and I get approached by a member of the Mayor's Political Advance team. To avoid embarrassing him, I will call him "John." When I was in Protective Operations, I would often conduct the protective site advance, ensuring our security plan was in place for the event the Mayor would attend. "John" would be there doing the political advance, talking with the person or persons the Mayor would meet with, going over the run of the show, meet and greets with other dignitaries at the event, things of that nature.

I hadn't seen him yet at the pier; it had been a while since we last spoke. We were both happy to see each other. I should explain, there was a sense of relief between people who hadn't seen each other in a while. The first interaction between people, seeing each other for the first time after 9/11, was "thank God, you made it." Many friends did not.

"John" and I have that exchange. We catch up quickly, and he is anxious to get something accomplished. What comes next, I couldn't get my head around.

At a very rapid pace, he tells me that he was happy to see me, not only because I made it, but also because I would be the only person he could think of who could help him out.

So, "John" tells me his plan.

"I have an idea, the Mayor and the Governor want to show the City is back to normal."

It's a few days after the 9/11 attacks. Smoke is still pouring out of the pile.

"Where are you going with this?" I ask him.

"The Mayor and Governor want to go fishing off the Pier. You are the only guy here who would understand this. I know you can get some fishing poles for them."

"Fishing poles so they can go fishing and show the City and the country that we are back to normal?"

"Exactly. Can you help?"

Multiple thoughts are colliding in my head. Does he have a concussion? Is he on any medication that could be causing this? Is this a quick onset of PTSD? Is he drunk?

Unfortunately for him, none of the above. This was "Johnny," who always did have a flair for "outside the box" thinking. But this was beyond even the wildest of thoughts.

Those of you who know me know that I have a devilish side. Sometimes I can't help myself. The only response I can offer is "Sure."

What comes next out of my mouth is ridiculous, and I think when he hears it from me, he will realize the absurdity of it all.

"So, I have a good idea. I have scuba divers inspecting the pier to ensure no bombs are being placed under it. I'll get a couple of fish and slip them to the divers before they go down. This way, when the Mayor and Governor drop the lines in the water, the divers can hook the fish on the lines and pull a bit. It will appear as if each caught a fish. I'll ensure they're the same size, so no measuring will be required. Sounds good?'

I can barely keep a straight face when I said it. He grabs my shoulder, leans in, and finishes the conversation.

"That's great! But make sure the fish are not frozen, the press will want to take pictures of them."

He thinks I am serious.

I tell him to ask the Mayor and the Governor when they want to do this. He should also ask the FEMA Director whether he wants to go fishing.

He shakes my hand and leaves, confident that we are all going fishing later that day.

I never did see him again after that. He just floated away as quickly as he floated in. Obviously, I never got the fishing poles, and I dared not bring them up with the Mayor.

That's what leadership looked like in those moments, an edited version of reality designed for television. They were managing optics, not outcomes.

I am sure the Mayor, Governor, President, and FEMA Director had no idea what was being asked in their name. No one would be that stupid. But the staff surrounding them is as much a part of the leadership problem. The race among staffers to be the first to tell the "boss" what is happening, without regard for accuracy, is a critical issue. The outcome of initial briefings after a crisis can make the most senior leaders appear either misinformed, asleep at the switch, or, worse, lying to the public. When the "Boss" is given bad information and runs with it, the results will be used by everyone who has it out for the "Boss." A perfect example of this was played out during a U.S. Senate hearing that questioned the FBI Director's competence.

Not long after the Charlie Kirk killing, Kash Patel, the FBI Director, was informed that a suspect had been arrested in connection with the shooting. He went on TV and announced the arrest. The suspect was subsequently released. Later, at a Senate Committee hearing, he was grilled on why he made that statement. The questioning focused on how misinformed he was and on his ability to lead the agency, given that one statement. It was political theater; nothing came of it, but it was said. He was trying to do the right thing and should be applauded for it. But others, such as politicians and some corporate leaders, take a different approach, They see blood in the water and act. The politics of the situation overrode the facts. Someone briefed him, possibly a little too quickly, and the facts were wrong.

That is one example of a leader getting bad information. But what about the leader who skews the facts for egotistical and political gain? Leaders who often have less insight than the national media make statements and promises that operational teams must live with.

The problem is that modern politics treats uncertainty like weakness. But in real crisis work, uncertainty is honesty. You can't lead without admitting what you don't know.

And those early decisions, made for television, can haunt operations for days. Kash Patel's actions were not malicious. What the Senators who grilled him and questioned his competence based on that fact was, in my opinion, malicious. They had time to prepare for the attack. At some point, I guess you can say it was a fair fight. He knew it was coming and prepared for it. They knew he was coming in and prepared to attack. That's politics.

But what is worse, in my opinion, is when a leader faces a crisis. No preparation for it, no proper understanding of the potential complexities of the events. They are flying by the seat of their pants, operating on the briefest of briefs from, hopefully, an expert on the subject. What this creates is political leadership, not operational leadership. Political leadership can be deadly. Why do they lead through the lens of politics?

The truth is, most politically driven leaders aren't malicious; they're afraid. They fear looking unprepared more than being unprepared. That fear drives poor communication. It causes them to promise safety they can't guarantee, assign blame before investigations are complete, and create enemies where none exist. In the intelligence world, we call that "decision pressure." In politics, it's called "Monday".

The irony is that during the worst moments, blackouts, shootings, and natural disasters, the public doesn't need a savior. They need someone to tell the truth. The human brain can process uncertainty; it can't process contradiction. When a leader says one thing and reality says another, trust collapses. Because once you lose public confidence in a crisis, you lose everything.

A great example of this is Hurricane Katrina, which hit New Orleans on August 29th, 2005. This one event, caused by the levee's failure, inundated the City by over 80%. The devastation included displacing over one million residents and caused over 1,400 deaths. During the mandatory evacuation period, the press interviewed residents and asked why they weren't leaving. The response was the same for many: "We are always told how bad it will be, but it never is." The people of New Orleans suffered from crisis fatigue; they were always told how bad it would be, but it never was. They lost faith in their leadership, and ultimately, because of this, some lost their lives.

After enough crises, you start to see patterns. The mistakes repeat like a bad script. It doesn't matter if it's a chemical leak, a blackout, a hurricane, or a security breach; the first hours always reveal the same disease: ego disguised as confidence.

Ego is the most contagious virus in leadership. It infects the entire chain of command. It starts when someone with power believes that being seen as decisive is more important than being correct. And once ego becomes operational policy, truth becomes collateral damage.

That's what leadership looked like in those moments, an edited version of reality designed for television. Regardless of the roles, they manage optics, not outcomes.

I used to think the problem was arrogance. Later, I realized it was fear. Politicians fear silence. It makes them look unsure. But the truth is, real leaders are comfortable with silence. They understand that credibility doesn't come from how fast you speak; it comes from how right you are when you finally do.

There's an old saying in crisis work: if you're the first one talking, you're probably wrong.

In the chaos of the first twenty-four hours, facts move more slowly than emotion. The data has to be confirmed, tested, and cross-checked. But emotion moves at the speed of broadcast. Today's news cycle has shrunk from 3 days to 24 hours to 8 hours. Once fear hits the public, no correction can outrun it.

That's why political leadership so often clashes with operational leadership. The leader's timeline is measured in press cycles; the responder's, in reality. You can work miracles in the field, but one sentence from the podium can undo it in seconds.

I learned to spot the warning signs. When a leader started a briefing with "Let me be clear," it usually meant they weren't. When they say "out of an abundance of caution," it means they have no plan. And when they declared "the situation is under control," it means they have no idea what was really happening.

That's not cynicism, it's experience.

The best leaders I've ever worked with didn't talk like politicians. They spoke like people. They asked questions before they gave answers. They didn't pretend to know everything. They told the truth, even when it wasn't pretty. Those are the people who earn credibility that lasts beyond the crisis.

But that kind of leadership is rare because it doesn't photograph well. The camera rewards confidence, not competence. The public sees a calm voice and assumes control. The reality is often a room full of exhausted people making decisions on bad information.

The public thinks leadership is about control. In reality, it's about connection, connecting people to the truth, even when it's uncomfortable.

During those first twenty-four hours, the most powerful thing a leader can say is *I don't know yet, but here's what we're doing to find out.* That sentence builds more trust than any confident lie ever could.

The problem is that honesty doesn't trend. Fear does. And that's why the first hours of every crisis are also the most dangerous, for truth, for trust, and for leadership itself.

We see it after hurricanes, after shootings, after any significant event. The same choreography played out: press conferences before facts, promises before plans, declarations before data. It wasn't about solving the problem; it was about being seen solving it.

That's not leadership. That's marketing.

The actual test of a leader isn't how they act once the cameras are rolling; it's how they behave when the cameras are gone. Real leaders check in with the people doing the work. They ask what's needed, not what sounds good. They focus on fixing the problem, not framing it.

Those first twenty-four hours reveal everything about a person's leadership philosophy. Some chase headlines. Others chase solutions. You can't do both.

In my years at OEM and later in consulting, I came to one conclusion that's as uncomfortable as it is universal: when politics drives the response, competence becomes optional. The people who actually help are the ones who quietly clean up after the press conferences end.

Leaders face internal conflicts over moral, legal, political, and personal gain issues. Your job is to know which one is driving the decisions, but recognize that at the base of it all, it's the ego.

That's why ego is so dangerous in a crisis. It replaces humility with performance. You stop listening to your experts because you're too busy scripting your next quote. And when leaders stop listening, systems collapse.

....

Leadership Principle:

- The first day of any crisis belongs to emotion. The second belongs to accountability. The leader's job is to survive both. Ego, fear, and optics can win you the first twenty-four hours, but they'll lose you the next twenty-four days.

PART 3
WHAT LEADERS SHOULD HAVE DONE

CHAPTER 10
WHAT CLASSIFIED AND CONFIDENTIAL REALLY MEAN

According to Merriam-Webster, Classified and Confidential are defined as follows.

"Classified": withheld from general circulation for reasons of national security.

"Confidential": intended for or restricted to the use of a particular person, group, or class.

When I first entered the NYPD Intelligence Division, I assumed classified meant dangerous, national secrets, espionage, real cloak-and-dagger stuff. I pictured folders stamped in red, guarded vaults, high-level clearance briefings. Being slightly facetious, but not by much, I found instead that people were classifying lunch schedules.

The term "classified" has been used and abused for a very long time. Conspiracy theorists will tell you the government classifies information so as not to let the public know what is really going on. Others will tell you it is vital to have national security secrets, for that exact reason, national security. My educational experiences have shown me it is somewhere in between. The definitions and concepts are malleable, making them easy to work with, whichever side you take.

At the National Security level, there is information that is genuinely a national secret, and its release can jeopardize lives. The ability to share information must be determined by who gets what, and there is a process to safeguard it. In the realm of intelligence operations, safeguarding sensitive information is paramount to maintaining operational security and protecting sources and methods.

I do believe there is information that needs to be treated as "national security" intelligence and should be kept "classified."

Precisely what is intelligence information, and where does it come from?

According to the US Naval War College, there are five sources of Intelligence information.

Human Intelligence (HUMINT) involves gathering information from human sources. This can be done openly, such as when FBI agents interview witnesses or suspects, or secretly through covert or espionage activities. The other four sources of intelligence are Signal Intelligence (SIGINT), Communications Intelligence (COMINT), Imagery Intelligence (IMINT), and Measurement and Signatures (MASINT). Open Source Intelligence (OSINT) is the fifth and one of the most widely used forms of intelligence today in non-governmental applications.

One key method for maintaining secrecy when handling classified information is the Sensitive Compartmented Information (SCI) system. SCI is an advanced classification level that goes beyond traditional security clearances by segregating intelligence into separate "compartments" or "codeword" categories. Each compartment contains highly sensitive data from specific intelligence sources, collection methods, or analytical processes, ensuring access is strictly controlled and granted only to individuals with a verified need-to-know.

This compartmentalization serves several essential purposes. By dividing intelligence into distinct compartments, agencies can reduce the risk of inadvertently exposing or compromising sensitive information. Even within a secure agency or department, not all personnel with high-level clearances will have access to every compartment. This need-to-know principle further limits the spread of intelligence, reducing vulnerabilities and safeguarding the identities of sources and operational methods. It also minimizes damage if an individual is compromised, as only information in their authorized compartments would be at risk.

To ensure the secure handling of SCI, specialized facilities called Sensitive Compartmented Information Facilities (SCIFs) are used. SCIFs provide a carefully designed, certified physical environment that prevents unauthorized access to or interception of sensitive discussions and documents. Electronic communications within and between SCIFs are governed by strict operational and technical controls, ensuring that SCI remains protected against espionage, eavesdropping, or cyber intrusions. Personnel authorized to enter SCIFs undergo thorough background checks and often receive additional training in secure information-handling procedures.

SCI compartmenting and SCIFs together form an advanced method for safeguarding intelligence. They carefully regulate access to highly sensitive information to protect sources and methods, maintain strategic advantages, and support national security. This complex, layered system is essential to modern intelligence activities, balancing the need to share critical information with the need to keep it secure.

While these stringent security measures protect intelligence operations from external threats, they also help define and limit the scope of intelligence activities themselves. The compartmentalization systems that restrict access to classified information work in tandem with legal frameworks that restrict where and how intelligence agencies can operate. Understanding these operational boundaries is crucial to dispelling widespread misconceptions about what intelligence agencies like the CIA are actually authorized to do, and equally important, what they are prohibited from doing within the United States.

Contrary to popular belief and a common misunderstanding, the Central Intelligence Agency is not authorized under Federal law to conduct surveillance on Americans living within the United States. The Agency is authorized to collect human intelligence outside the United States, as are other intelligence groups within other American agencies. Another misconception about the CIA is that its intelligence collectors have law-enforcement powers, like those of an FBI Special Agent. This is not the case. CIA Case Officers lack the authority to make arrests; they are not Special Agents. Those whom the average person would consider an "Agent" are technically "Case Officers." Agents are the people who provide information to the Agency.

These legal and operational distinctions highlight the formal boundaries that govern intelligence work, but they also underscore an important reality: much of the information intelligence agencies need doesn't require clandestine collection. While Case Officers abroad recruit and handle human sources, and while compartmented intelligence protects the most sensitive operations, the intelligence community has increasingly recognized that vast amounts of valuable information exist in plain sight, freely accessible to anyone with the knowledge and tools to find it. This realization has elevated the importance of a collection discipline that operates entirely outside the world of classified sources and covert methods.

Open-Source Intelligence (OSINT) encompasses a wide range of information and sources available to the general public. A significant source of intelligence data comes from open-source writings and posts. Estimates indicate that 90% of classified material can be found in open sources, such as newspapers, magazines, websites, social media, think tank reports, and other sources.

According to Lieutenant General (ret) Samuel V. Wilson, former director of the Defense Intelligence Agency (DIA), "Ninety percent of intelligence comes from open sources. The other 10 percent, the clandestine work, is just the more dramatic. The real intelligence hero is Sherlock Holmes, not James Bond."

An Intelligence Analyst is, as General Wilson described, the Sherlock Holmes. The analyst will gather all of the information, read through it, and write a report, in essence a term paper, on whatever topic he or she is writing about. Guess what happens to the report that is created? It becomes "classified." Material that was previously open to everyone appears in a report that is now classified and therefore cannot be shared. Does anybody else here see the irony in this?

At the National level, there is a clearly defined need within national security. But not everyone is working under such tight restrictions. Using "classified" or "Confidential" to control information dissemination in non-national-security matters renders it a weapon. The two words are often used interchangeably. It is a shroud used to hide behind. In every job or association with any intelligence group I was ever a part of, there's been one universal truth: the more someone says, "That's classified or confidential," the less they actually know or are willing to share. Not because it is truly secret, but more often than not, it played out hidden as power. If information is power, then having secrets makes you very powerful. Poor leaders use this power to their advantage.

"Confidential" means whatever the speaker needs it to mean. Sometimes it means sensitive, sometimes it means personal, and most of the time it boils down to two things. The first is "I don't want to look stupid," so if I say it's classified or confidential, I don't have to say anything and can just claim I have no idea. The second is more devious. In this context, it means that if I disclose the information, you will know what I know and can use that to your advantage. As we have seen before, what drives this is the ego. An ego needs power, and having information no one else has is the most potent power trip an executive can have.

The same pattern shows up everywhere, from federal task forces to city departments to boardrooms. Leaders hoard information because it makes them feel indispensable. The logic was simple: if you know what I know, I'm replaceable.

That is the hidden fear behind every locked drawer and encrypted file, the fear of irrelevance.

At one meeting, an executive once told me, "We can't give them everything. We need to protect our value." I told him, "If your value depends on secrecy, you don't have value, you have a secret."

He didn't like that answer. Most people in power don't.

What "classified" really meant, I learned, was comfort. Comfort in control, comfort in hierarchy, comfort in never having to admit you didn't have the answers. It is a shield used by people who fear being questioned.

That's how incompetence survives: it hides behind clearance levels, both perceived and real.

Early on, I realized how the term "confidential" could be weaponized; it wasn't about protection; it was about exclusion. It was theater, designed to remind everyone who had the bigger "S" for Superman on his chest.

I was newly assigned to the Intelligence Division and asked to provide an escort for a dignitary in need of protection. He was not of the stature of a country leader, but he was of sufficient standing that threats against him required protection. The protective detail consisted of about 6 of us. Usually, we get a briefing before departing for the escort. The brief typically covered what was happening, where we were going, locations, and all the information we would need. Tonight was going to be a little different. We were told at the briefing to go to our lockers and get our big guns. This was at a time when the department was still using revolvers; semi-automatics did not come into use until later. Most of us would carry the smaller .38-caliber revolver rather than the service weapon, which had a 4-inch barrel. We looked at each other and asked, Why?

We were told that we could not be told the why; it was "confidential." We needed to get them, and we would have to stand for inspection to ensure we had them.

We requested the threat information and any details on how the attack could occur. Was the threat from a bomb, a gun, or a drive-by? Just what was the threat? Were there pictures of the potential attacker? We were told that we couldn't be told the why, just do it. Feeling like lambs heading out to slaughter, we complied but spent the entire shift on edge. It wasn't until we returned to the command that we began to relax and breathe normally.

We never really found out what the threat was, but the boss who sent us out felt proud that he kept a secret and had the power to make it happen. That was not leadership, that was ego personified.

Corporate America has the same egomaniacal lunatics in its ranks. It should learn from the U.S. military.

The military leadership concept is simple: *train upward.* Every person on a team should be able to replace the person above them. That's how you build resilience. It's also how you build trust. If your people understand what you know, they can make decisions when you're not there.

Corporate America does the reverse. It trains downward, teaches just enough for the job, never enough to replace the boss. It's a system built on insecurity. The fear of being outshone undermines initiative more quickly than any external threat.

That difference explains why military operations often adapt under pressure, while bureaucracies collapse. In one, the mission drives the hierarchy. In the other, the hierarchy drives the mission. When information is shared freely, leaders multiply their capability. When it's restricted, they multiply their liability.

Every "need to know" restriction is a future bottleneck waiting to happen. And in crisis management, bottlenecks cost time, and time costs lives.

I've seen the aftermath of that failure too many times. A manager refuses to brief subordinates "until the situation is clearer," only for the situation to escalate while everyone waits for permission to act. Or an executive hides a vulnerability report to protect the stock price until the breach becomes public. When the truth finally surfaces, it's never the lack of information that hurts; it's the proof that someone had it and chose not to share. The cover-up is always worse than the event itself.

That's how trust dies. Quietly, internally, one withheld fact at a time.

Leadership transparency isn't about reckless disclosure. It's about context. Good leaders explain the *why* behind the limits. They don't just say "you can't know"; they say "here's why this stays internal for now." That single step turns restriction into respect. Because here's the reality: people will accept what they don't like, but not what they don't understand.

When I started PCC Secure, I built the company around that idea. Every training program, every threat assessment, every client engagement was designed to demystify the process. We teach not only the rules but also the reasoning behind them. We think like analysts, observe, question, verify, and explain because a person who understands the "why" behind a protocol will consistently outperform one who only memorizes it.

That's the antidote to the classified mindset: education. The more people you empower to understand, the fewer you'll have to manage.

Too many leaders think keeping information locked away makes them indispensable. It doesn't. It makes them a liability. If your organization can't function without you, you haven't built a team; you've built a dependency.

And dependency is not leadership; it's ego management. When I look back on my years in private industry, I realize that the classified culture was almost always about personal security, not about national or corporate security. The fear of being exposed, replaced, or questioned influences more decisions than any policy ever will. The same applies in business, media, and even personal relationships. The instinct to withhold is universal; the courage to share isn't.

That is why transparency is the ultimate test of leadership. It forces leaders to rely on competence rather than concealment. Those who are confident in their skills are willing to teach, explain, and share what they know, because their value does not depend on secrecy. Leaders who resist teaching often mistake protection for proficiency, when in reality it signals insecurity. In the end, leadership is not defined by what one hides behind, but by what 1 is willing to give away.

This principle of transparency in teaching and knowledge sharing stands in stark contrast to the careful control of information we've discussed throughout this chapter. Yet the tension between openness and secrecy extends beyond organizational leadership into the public sphere, where questions of what should remain classified and what the public has a right to know become matters of democratic debate. Perhaps nowhere is this tension more evident, or more contentious, than in the relationship between the intelligence community, or corporate leaders, and the news media, where the controlled release, authorized disclosure, and unauthorized leak of sensitive information intersect with First Amendment freedoms and the public's need to understand government operations.

This chapter would not be complete if I did not mention the press and their use of "confidential" information and the release of "classified" material.

I have respect for the press and the service they provide. But I have to question: do they sometimes overstep the line between the public's right to know and the release of information that could be detrimental to an investigation or to national security? Is that line sometimes overstepped not for true "public right to know," but for the reporter's selfish reasons to get a scoop and further his or her career? How about the collateral damage that occurs when certain stories come to light? Who takes responsibility for these victims?

As a Detective working on homicide cases with a press following, I sometimes found this a horrible distraction. Sensitive case information developed by the media and released can significantly hinder an investigation. And when questioned about it, the answer always seems the same. The public has a right to know. But do they? I can agree that they have a right to know, but should they?

I had a great friend, who I lost this year to pancreatic cancer, Jim Henry, who has a saying he may have borrowed, but in honor of him, I will attribute it to him: "Because you can, doesn't mean you should."

I define it as a right to know, not a must-know.

This creates a yin-yang dynamic between the investigators and the press, who argue that the public has a right to know. Does the public have a need and right to know during the investigation? That question has been debated for centuries, and I am not sure it will ever be settled. I believe the public has the right to know, but not while the investigation is ongoing. That is what trials are for. The cases can be jeopardized, and lives can be put at risk. It frustrates me when you see a reporter or group of reporters do everything they can to report on a story for their own selfish reasons, only to hide behind the line, "the public has a right to know." Bullshit. Pure and simple.

More often than not, a negotiation must take place between the reporter and the Commander to delay publication of the story. Reporters are promised the first news so they can be the first to report. It is a nasty form of extortion that gets played out daily. When the stories are published, the sources remain "confidential."

....

Leadership Principles:

- Every leader faces the same choice: protect your position or protect your people. One depends on secrecy; the other depends on trust. When you choose secrecy, you create followers. When you choose trust, you create leaders.

- If you want to lead through chaos, remember, clarity is your only real advantage. The moment you start classifying everything, you're no longer managing information. You're managing fear.

CHAPTER 11
MANAGING PERSONALITIES – THE STUPID, INCOMPETENT, AND MANIPULATIVE

You can build the best plan in the world, and it'll still fall apart the moment the wrong personality walks into the room. In crisis management, I used to think the enemy was chaos. Then I realized it was people who created it. Not the bad guys outside the fence, the ones inside. Over the years, I learned to group them into three categories: stupid, incompetent, and manipulative. Each one can derail an operation in their own way.

The one lesson few teach in leadership is the human factor, how to deal with stupidity. As the comedian Ron White says, you can't fix stupid. You can train, budget, and prepare all you want, but sooner or later, you'll have to lead people who make bad decisions for reasons that have nothing to do with inexperience or lack of skill. According to Merriam-Webster dictionary, it is defined as "acting in an unintelligent or careless manner." Whatever the definition, it is easier to be politically incorrect, blunt, and say they are just stupid. There is also a lack of common sense in their actions. And we all know that common sense isn't common anymore.

An example of how stupidity can play out and cause a crisis occurred during a response in Queens, NY, amid heightened alerts for potential chemical attacks. As the story goes, there was a fraud investigation involving thousands of dollars in unpaid chemicals. Police responded to a home in the Douglaston section and gained access to the residence. Once inside, they discovered what appeared to be a chemistry lab. In the basement, they found a silver canister labeled "SARIN," along with other materials, including ether, nitromethane, and containers marked "radioactive."

When questioned, the homeowner, a 52-year-old male described by neighbors as a "chemistry buff," said the label was a joke. Just oxygen, he said. Nothing dangerous.

Whether he found it funny became irrelevant the moment responders saw the label. This was 1997, just two years after the Tokyo subway attack, in which sarin gas killed thirteen people and injured thousands. The fear was real. The threat was credible. And now the response was in motion.

Over 200 people were evacuated from the surrounding neighborhood. The NYPD Emergency Service Unit and the Fire Department Hazmat Team responded. Eventually, the Department of Defense also got involved. Streets were blocked. Families were displaced. Resources were mobilized across multiple agencies.

All because someone thought it would be clever to label a canister "sarin" as a joke.

It didn't matter whether the container actually held oxygen. It didn't matter whether the homeowner meant no harm. The moment that label existed, the crisis became real. A careless act, someone thinking they were being funny, caused trauma, chaos, and massive resource deployment across an entire neighborhood.

That's the problem with stupidity. It doesn't have to be malicious to be dangerous. It just has to be thoughtless. And in a world already on edge, thoughtlessness can be catastrophic.

But the homeowner's stupidity wasn't the only problem that day. Once multiple agencies arrived on scene, a different kind of chaos erupted, the kind that happens when egos collide and nobody wants to back down. The Fire Department believed it was responsible because hazardous materials were involved. The NYPD believed it was their job because it was terrorism and a possible crime scene. This was almost a complete replay of the cyanide debacle.

While leadership fought over jurisdiction, the people actually doing the work had to figure out how to function in an impossible situation.

To go "down range," as we would say, you needed personal protective equipment. The protective gear is known as a Level "A" hazmat suit. It resembles a large moon suit. It is challenging to navigate in and must remain sealed to provide protection. Carrying and possibly using a weapon in a suit not designed for this purpose was ill-advised. The NYPD officers had a workaround. They would cut a hole in the suit's hand and duct-tape the opening closed. The Fire Department went crazy, and they were right.

Eventually, that chaos was sorted out. Arrangements were made to purchase a casket for the cylinder, which was then removed and sent to the U.S. military lab for examination. The lab tests were negative for SARIN, and the whole city felt much better.

Dealing with individuals who act without sufficient thought or judgment poses a unique and significant challenge during a crisis. These individuals are frequently the most common in any group, and their actions can be more dangerous than those of outright malicious actors or those who deliberately withhold information. They mean well, driven often by a sincere desire to contribute or to be decisive. Still, their lack of critical thinking leads them to make impulsive decisions that exacerbate problems rather than resolve them. In crises where every action can have amplified consequences, this impulsivity not only hinders their effectiveness but also jeopardizes others' safety. We saw this in the cyanide and "Sarin" responses.

For the person acting without sufficient forethought, the consequences of this "stupidity" are profound. Charging into high-risk situations without proper equipment or preparation not only exposes oneself to harm but also imposes additional burdens on others who must rescue or cover for them. Similarly, disseminating unverified information spreads confusion and panic, undermining the reliability of communication channels vital to coordinated response efforts. Their confusion of speed with leadership, and their valuing of rushed decisions over thoughtful ones, often lead to missteps and missed opportunities to achieve practical solutions.

From a leadership perspective, dealing with such behavior is doubly difficult. A leader must manage not only the tangible challenges of the crisis but also the unpredictable and sometimes chaotic effects of well-intentioned yet impulsive team members. Stupid actions dilute the clarity of command, forcing leaders to divert time and resources to contain or correct preventable errors. Worse, this behavior can erode trust within the team; others may become frustrated or demoralized when reckless actions lead to setbacks or increased risk. Strong leaders understand that leadership isn't about rushing to be first but about making wise decisions under pressure, balancing decisiveness with accuracy.

Ultimately, the presence of individuals who act without thinking requires leaders to foster a culture of calm, disciplined assessment, even in the most stressful moments. Training, clear communication, and accountability are crucial for mitigating the damage such behavior can cause. Recognizing that those who act impulsively often do so with good intent, leaders must channel their energy constructively, ensuring that decisiveness is coupled with informed judgment and that speed does not compromise safety or mission success. Managing "stupidity" is less about reprimand and more about guiding thoughtful action, transforming potential liabilities into assets in crisis response.

While stupidity creates immediate chaos through thoughtless action, incompetence creates a slower poison, one that corrodes from within.

The incompetent occupy positions they never should've had. They lack the skills but have the title, usually because someone above them liked how they talked in meetings. The incompetent doesn't make quick mistakes; they make slow, corrosive ones. They delay, overanalyze, and create committees when decisions are needed. They crave direction but resist accountability. The best way to manage them is to set short, measurable deadlines and document everything. You can't rely on performance; you rely on proof.

Unfortunately, I have a client who is incompetent in every way. There are times I swear he wins the trifecta: he can be stupid, incompetent, and manipulative all at once. Let me show you what all three look like in one person.

He is a senior executive at a publicly traded company. I have been with this company for a long time. I have observed many executives in training advance through the ranks, and he was consistently regarded as a rising star. I always believed he was being brought along too fast. He lacked maturity, which was likely his most significant weakness. As he rose, it became clear to everyone that he was being promoted because someone high in the organization believed he was the future. The more they promoted him within the company and through industry awards, the more he began to believe his own press. Believing in your own headlines feeds the ego, and we know what happens when the ego gets out in front.

When looking back, the pattern would be easy to miss. He was not fast to make decisions and made no quick mistakes. He requested more and more work, always the first to jump in and volunteer for whatever came up. Initially, he was an ideal employee, someone you wanted on your team. As time went on, the wheels started to come off the wagon. Projects were delayed. Meetings were cancelled and never rescheduled. He would never make the decision; he would always look to others to tell him what to do next. His management style was to wait until the last minute and get direction from the "experts" around him. It reached the point where we all realized he was just plainly incompetent and afraid to make a decision. Emails and phone calls remain unanswered until a crisis arises.

You might ask yourself, does this ever catch up with the person? Like most organizations, if you are politically stuck with a person, the best you can do is promote him to get him out of your hair and make it someone else's problem.

But the worst are the *manipulative*. They know precisely what they're doing. They see every crisis as an opportunity for leverage: budget, power, recognition. While everyone else is trying to fix the problem, they're calculating how to benefit from it.

You can spot them by their timing. They're quiet until the moment a decision looks unpopular, then suddenly they're not in the room. When something succeeds, they're the first to take credit. Manipulative leaders are adept at invoking plausible deniability.

I was working as a law enforcement controller for an exercise conducted by the U.S. Department of Justice. It was a terrorism exercise being conducted in multiple locations around the country, known as "Top-Off." The name is derived from the senior government officials who participated in the exercises. The area I was in had a simulated biological attack in which there would be a multi-agency response: local Police, State Police, and the FBI. To "control" the exercise, an FBI agent served as the "Federal Controller" and a player in the exercise. He was a dorky-looking individual who had not one, but two radios slung across his chest and carried the pre-requisite clipboard. For the purpose of this book, I'll call him "Sheldon."

The exercise begins with a report of a foul odor reportedly coming from a "hotel." The 9-1-1 call goes in, and the local Police Department responds. When they arrived, things became very interesting.

The first Officers walked into the hotel and into the room where we simulated a dead body lying in bed. In preparation for the exercise and to simulate the biological component, we spread Limburger cheese on the windowsill, the nightstand, and the dummy lying in bed. That gave us the "foul smell." Once they observed the issue, they backed out and called for a supervisor. He responds, takes a look, and calls the Captain. Now the Captain shows up and declares it a terrorist event. "Sheldon" had it set up that the local

Police would play with this for hours and never make a decision. He further anticipated that the locals would argue with the State Police for hours over who is in charge, possibly involving Health Department officials, and that it would drag on for a long while. All of this started around 9 am. The exercise was scheduled to continue until about 5 pm. What was not anticipated was the Captain's actions. The exercise came to an abrupt halt.

A time-out was called, and a meeting was held with all parties involved. "Sheldon" jumps into the middle of the circle and tells the Captain that he needs to fix this. It is his responsibility. What came next, I chuckle to myself, and must admit I was so proud of that Captain. He looked "Sheldon" in the eye and said, "No."

"Sheldon" tells the group that he had it set up. The locals need to run the exercise until approximately 3 pm, when the FBI evidence recovery team will arrive and take over. He planned the whole thing to make himself and the Bureau appear heroic. What he got was a kick in the nether regions of his loins. To try to save face, he proclaims that once the scene is considered a terrorist event, the locals would lose all control. The FBI was now in control, and the locals had no say in the matter. "Sheldon" looks into the eyes of the Captain.

"You sure you want to lose all control and turn it over to the FBI?"

The Captain's response almost brought a round of applause from the group around him.

"It's terrorism, it's yours, have a nice day."

"Sheldon" had no other option but to call for the Evidence Recovery Team. According to his plan, they would be there later in the day. Now they had to scramble to get a team together and get them there quickly. It didn't happen so fast.

"Sheldon" wasn't just manipulative; he designed an exercise to make himself the hero. When reality didn't cooperate, his entire plan collapsed because it was built on ego rather than outcomes.

During my time with the NYPD, I was honored to join the elite Hostage Negotiation Team. I began to understand these personalities more deeply. Negotiation teaches you to listen for motive and emotion, not just words. Every person has a reason for their behavior, even if they don't admit it. Some seek control, some seek validation, some seek to stop feeling powerless.

In hostage negotiation training, we studied how to listen with precision. The goal wasn't to agree with the subject; it was to understand what was driving them. Every phrase, pause, and tone revealed whether they were scared, angry, or simply posturing. Once you knew which one it was, you could choose the correct response: empathy for fear, structure for anger, distance for manipulation.

That same logic applies to leadership. The people who derail organizations aren't random; they're predictable. If you can identify which type you're dealing with, you can neutralize the damage before it spreads.

The same psychology applies to leadership. Stupid, incompetent, and manipulative behavior all stem from fear, fear of failure, exposure, or irrelevance. Once you understand that, you stop taking it personally and start managing it strategically.

In the field, that meant learning when to push, when to pause, and when to step back. Sometimes the best move was letting someone fail safely so they could see the consequences. At other times, it meant documenting everything because the manipulative individual always attempts to rewrite history to cover their tracks.

One of the hardest lessons I learned in leadership was that not every battle is worth fighting. You can't fix stupidity with yelling and screaming, incompetence with pressure, or manipulation with confrontation. What you can do is recognize the type early and adjust your strategy. Pick the hills you are willing to die on, carefully.

Skill and competence are undeniably essential in leadership and professional growth. They can be taught, refined, and assessed through intentional training, practice, and feedback. Whether it's developing a technical skill, learning effective communication, or honing strategic decision-making, skill development follows a straightforward process: instruction, repetition, and evaluation. Leaders can invest in training programs, workshops, or mentoring systems to enhance their teams' capabilities, knowing that time and effort will yield appreciable improvements. This is the relatively straightforward part of leadership development.

Integrity, however, belongs to a different realm. It is a character trait deeply rooted in one's values, principles, and moral sense. Unlike skill, integrity can't be taught through a training session or a checklist. It comes from an individual's internal compass, their honesty, accountability, and ethical consistency, even when no one is watching. Integrity is tested not during easy times but in moments of challenge, pressure, or temptation. Leaders with integrity are those who choose to do the right thing, even if it may cost them personally or professionally.

The distinction between skill and integrity is crucial because skills without integrity can lead to harmful consequences. A highly skilled leader who lacks integrity may manipulate systems, exploit people, or pursue self-interest at the expense of the organization's core values and mission. Conversely, a leader with unwavering integrity but developing skills can grow into an effective leader who earns trust, inspires loyalty, and fosters a culture of openness and respect. Ultimately, leadership is about who you are as much as what you can do; training can improve abilities, but only character determines how those abilities are used.

For organizations, this distinction underscores the importance of recruiting and developing leaders through a dual lens, prioritizing both innate integrity and skill development. While skill gaps can be filled with time and education, integrity is the foundation on which leadership rests. Without it, leadership breaks down. Leaders who demonstrate integrity create environments where transparency flourishes, ethical conduct is standard, and teams feel confident in their direction. In a world where trust is a fragile and precious commodity, the adage "You can train skill; you can't train integrity" remains a timeless reminder of what truly matters in leadership.

That realization changed how I lead my teams. I no longer expect everyone to operate from the same moral compass. I began to focus on predictability rather than perfection, understanding how people would respond under stress and planning accordingly.

That's what leadership really is: managing human behavior under abnormal conditions. The policies, the plans, the protocols, they're the easy part. The hard part is doing all that while surrounded by egos, fear, and ambition.

Leadership isn't about managing operations; it's about controlling behavior. You don't lead tasks; you lead people, and people come with motives, insecurities, and blind spots that no manual can fix.

I learned that most leadership breakdowns aren't failures of knowledge or resources. They're failures of emotional intelligence, the inability to read the room, sense intent, and adjust accordingly. The more power someone gains, the more likely they are to forget that leadership is a behavioral skill, not a technical one.

As a consultant, brought in to advise leadership on crises, I learned that not every conflict you face has to be won. Sometimes you win; sometimes you document and step aside to limit your liability. As I've said before, *insurance isn't for when you're right; it's for when you're wrong*. There are leaders who will ask for your professional opinion solely to validate their actions. Recognize, these are the manipulative ones.

Early in my leadership career, I tried to "save" everyone. I thought effective leaders could address poor behavior through mentorship. But experience taught me a harder truth: you can only help people who want to be helped. Everyone else is a liability waiting to mature.

That's why documentation matters. In every major organization I've ever worked with, government, corporate, or private security, the strongest leaders are also the best record-keepers. They don't write things down for bureaucracy; they write things down to survive history. When chaos hits, memory becomes negotiation.

Good leaders learn to manage liability the same way they manage risk. You can't eliminate it, but you can reduce exposure. That means training your team to think, documenting your warnings, and recognizing when walking away is the most intelligent decision. Understanding personality isn't just about self-protection; it's about operational efficiency. When you understand what drives people, you can create an environment that absorbs their weaknesses rather than collapsing under them. You stop fighting human nature and start leveraging it.

That's the real art of leadership through chaos. You can't force people to be better than they are. Minimizing the knee-jerk reaction produces the least long-term damage. This is accomplished using the technique I describe in the next chapter. As I learned in the Hostage Negotiation Team, slow things down in a crisis.

And that's how you win, by managing people, not pretending they're something they're not.

....

Leadership Principles:

- Recognizing a person's personality types and emotional drivers provides insight into the causes and effects that must be managed.

- Know the difference between when you are working through the chaos of the situation and when you are managing the chaos created by the people around you.

CHAPTER 12
THE "STOP" TECHNIQUE

*"Five percent of the people think; Ten percent
of the people think they think; and the other
eighty-five percent would rather die than think."*
—Thomas A. Edison

Edison understood something most leaders ignore: the instinct to act is natural, but the discipline to think is learned. That is what the STOP technique teaches.

Every mistake I've ever seen in leadership started the same way: people not thinking.

Most people think leadership is about speed, making decisions quickly, acting decisively, and reacting before others. That's what gets you promoted, noticed, and quoted. But in a crisis, speed kills. The faster you move, the more likely you are to trip over something you didn't see coming. What you knee-jerk to now will cause another crisis you have to contend with. The knee-jerk reaction to that causes yet another crisis. Eventually, you get so far down range in the crises you've created that you almost forget what got you there in the first place.

I was teaching a course on threat recognition and behavior analysis. The behavior a person exhibits is as telling as if they explained their intentions verbally. You can learn a lot just from watching. Surveillance techniques have been used by the old-time criminal profession of "pickpocketing." A pickpocket doesn't just walk up to you to take your wallet or valuables. He watches you for a while. How would he know your money was in your front pocket, or your wallet was inside your jacket breast pocket? Because you "tell" him by your actions.

In counterterrorism, monitoring the behavior of bad actors seeking to harm is called "Hostile Surveillance Detection." I teach how to identify subtle behavioral signs associated with criminal intent, indicators like how someone carries a bomb or repeatedly taps the area where they're carrying a gun. The best way to find that person is to use the "STOP" technique.

Before taking my class outside for simulation drills, I always gave them a practice exercise. The exercise was simple: identify suspicious activity before it escalates. To make it engaging, I provided them with a scenario.

"What if someone wanted to blow up Cinderella's Castle?" I asked. "How would they do it?"

What happened next changed how I taught leadership forever.

Immediately, the room came alive. Everyone jumped straight to the attack, where the suspect would stand, how they'd get the bomb in, and how the crowd would react.

I let them go for a few minutes, then stopped them mid-sentence.

"Go back," I said.

They looked confused. "Go back where?"

"To before the explosion," I said. "Walk it backward. Step by step."

Reluctantly, they began tracing the story backward from the moment of the explosion. It wasn't easy to keep them on track. It never is. They want to get from start to finish as quickly as possible. That's human nature.

They were happy with, "I'd make a bomb, bring it to the Castle, lay it down, and blow it up."

So I asked, "How many behaviors did you get to see? How many opportunities were there to spot the person?"

There were very few in their scenario. I forced them to start at the point of the explosion and consider the exact behavior leading up to it, seconds before the blast. Then the seconds before that. Breaking the event down into brief moments, working backwards. The frustration they were feeling was palpable. Somewhere, it became a game. The competition among the class members grew increasingly intense.

Within ten minutes, the entire tone of the room changed. They went from guessing outcomes to identifying behaviors, from speculation to analysis. At each identified point, there was an opportunity to observe the suspect's actions and stop the attack.

When we finished, I told them, "You just learned how to lead."

The room laughed, but I wasn't joking. What they'd done in that exercise, stopping, tracking backward, observing behaviors, and planning, is precisely what leaders fail to do under pressure. They rush forward because stillness is perceived as weakness. But the truth is, control lives in the pause.

Building the Foundation

Those classes became the foundation for the STOP Technique: a four-step process for reversing failure thinking. It's not a theory, it's a discipline.

I started testing it on real cases. After every incident, I'd sit with my team and work backward from the outcome. Whether it was a security lapse, a communication failure, or a leadership mistake, the question was always the same: *Where did this start to go wrong?*

Sometimes the answer was technical: a missed alert, a faulty radio. More often, it was human, a rushed assumption, an ignored warning, an ego-driven shortcut. By walking it backward, we could pinpoint the exact moment where clarity gave way to chaos.

Assumptions are not allowed. There's a famous saying about making assumptions, not sure who to credit for it, but it's become part of our lexicon: *"Never assume, because when you do, you make an ass out of you and me."*

In the rush to reach the end of a scenario, we make assumptions about what we believe will happen. When one of them fails, the event changes. That one change might trigger a crisis you now have to address.

Understanding the Enemy: Cognitive Bias

In leadership, it's not enough to find the mistake; you have to see *why you made it.* One of the main culprits is a psychological effect called cognitive bias.

What is cognitive bias? Cognitive bias influences how we interpret the world, pushing us to read new information through the lens of what we already believe and have experienced. When that happens, our conclusions can drift away from reality without us realizing it.

We also rely on heuristics, mental shortcuts that help us categorize information and guide how we process and respond to it. These shortcuts enable quick decisions but also contribute to cognitive biases.

We take shortcuts based on previous knowledge. If I encounter a situation that's similar to another experience I've had, I may behave in the same way.

If I believe I have experience in a given area, I can readily apply it to the current crisis. While expertise is generally helpful, one must be careful to distinguish experience from ego.

The STOP Technique works because it attacks the two enemies of sound decision-making: ego and momentum. Ego makes you defend a bad idea; momentum makes you double down on it. Stopping breaks both.

The irony is that it's not new. The Marines have been doing it for decades. They call it "after-action analysis." Engineers call it "root cause review." Pilots call it "checklist discipline." The only difference is that I made it both emotional and procedural.

Whether you're managing a counterterrorism operation or overseeing a construction site, every poor response to a crisis ends with the words, "I thought we had it." When the "Monday morning quarterbacking" begins, it's essentially the same as using the STOP technique, pausing to review and analyze what happened. The key difference is that by engaging in this reflective process early, before others start questioning you, you take control of the situation. The STOP technique is designed to help prevent regret and misjudgment, making it clear why it's essential to pause and evaluate first rather than waiting to be questioned later.

Over the years, I have used it everywhere, from emergency management drills to private client assessments to executive training. I'd watch the same transformation happen. The moment people slowed down and worked backward, their vision sharpened. They stopped arguing and started thinking.

It's the most powerful leadership tool I've ever used, and the simplest.

But simplicity doesn't mean easy.

Because the hardest thing in the world for a leader to do isn't act, it's to stop.

Breaking Down the STOP Technique

The STOP Technique became my anchor point, an antidote to chaos disguised as simplicity. It's built on four steps: **Stop, Track, Observe, Plan.** It sounds like common sense until you try to apply it in real time, when alarms are sounding, radios are screaming, and everyone around you is waiting for a decision. Let's break it down into its parts.

Stop

It begins with the most challenging part: pausing. In a crisis, everything pushes you forward: adrenaline, fear, public pressure, and ego. People equate motion with leadership. They think "doing something" is better than "doing nothing." That mindset destroys more plans than failure ever could.

Stopping means taking ownership of the timeline. You control the pace; the situation doesn't. When you stop, you reclaim thinking space. You separate emotion from fact.

I tell clients: "If you can't stop, you can't see." That pause is where situational awareness is born.

As a member of the NYPD Hostage Negotiation Team, I was taught to deliberately slow things down during hostage or barricade situations, which closely parallels the "STOP" technique: pause to assess and control a situation before reacting. Just as the negotiation team uses time to de-escalate tension and build communication, the STOP technique encourages individuals to pause before reacting impulsively, reflect on the situation, and make more informed decisions. Both approaches recognize that rushing can escalate conflict or lead to mistakes, while slowing down creates space for better judgment and effective problem-solving.

By intentionally pausing, whether in a high-stakes negotiation or in everyday decision-making, individuals gain the opportunity to gather information, manage emotions, and consider potential consequences. This measured pace increases the likelihood of peaceful resolutions and reduces the chance of regretful actions. In essence, the NYPD's HNT strategy and the STOP technique both leverage time to transform reactive responses into thoughtful, intentional actions that promote safety and positive outcomes. That's leadership through a crisis.

Track

Once you stop, you track. Walk the event backward from the outcome to the decision points that led to it. Every crisis has breadcrumbs. You follow them in reverse to see how each choice influenced the next.

Tracking forces accountability. You can't hide behind excuses when the path is right in front of you. It also reveals the differences between what might happen and what people think could happen.

A great example of this came one day while I was teaching a group of law enforcement officers the "STOP" technique. During the class, I used an intelligence report as an example that described a potential attack at a mall. I asked the class what they would do if they were the Chief. What's your plan to identify the person or persons and stop the attack?

Quickly, they started where all classes go, right to the end.

Suggestions ranged from putting marked units in the parking lot to driving around to spot the attackers before the attack. Others discussed placing officers in mall stores to increase visibility and potentially deter the attack. Nearly all of them discussed how the event would proceed during the attack. This was expected.

I asked, "What about the behaviors leading up to the event? What could you observe well before the attack that you aren't seeing?"

Thus began the long, arduous task of walking them through the event in reverse. For brevity, I will cut most of the conversation.

Let's start with the actual attack, I said. "How does that happen?"

"The gunman rides in a car that pulls up fast, he gets out with a rifle and runs into the store shooting."

"You realize your plan is like catching lightning in a bottle," I asked. "Let's track this back from that point."

During the backward tracking, it was identified that the subjects had likely engaged in active surveillance. Behaviors included how to enter the parking lot, where to park, where the surveillance cameras were located, and how their positions were documented.

Tracking doesn't assign blame; it exposes friction points before they recur.

Observe

Next comes **Observe**, the discipline of seeing without judging. You analyze every layer: behavior, communication, systems, timing. Observation is the process of separating assumptions from facts. It's also the area where ego can creep in.

Observation also takes into account emotions. You don't just watch what happened; you watch how people reacted. Fear, anger, pride, and indecision are data points, too. In the intelligence world, we say that everything, regardless of how small or irrelevant, *is intelligence information.*

In the mall scenario, there was significant potential for hostile surveillance detection intelligence that could have been used before the attack, all of which would have been missed if it hadn't been broken down and the possible event tracked.

Observation teaches humility. You realize that systems don't fail because of one person; they fail because everyone assumes someone else is thinking.

Plan

The final step, **Plan**, is where you build forward from what you've learned. It's not just about preventing the last mistake; it's about designing systems that adapt to new ones.

Planning within the STOP framework is deliberate rather than reactive. You plan with hindsight in mind. You ask, "If this happens again, what changes will make this impossible or less damaging?"

In crisis management, we use the "STOP" framework to develop a plan for responding to a situation without causing further harm. In the mall scenario, a plan was designed to provide the best opportunity to obtain an early warning of potential developments and to prevent the attack. All the officers agreed that their actions would have been to set up counter-surveillance teams.

When people know *why* they're doing something, not just *how,* chaos slows down.

The Human Side of STOP

"STOP" isn't just a leadership model; it's a behavioral reset. It rewires the instinct to react. It permits people to think.

The first time I taught it to corporate executives, I could see the same look I'd seen in cops and first responders years earlier: resistance. They didn't want to slow down. They thought speed equaled control. Subsequently, we participated in a crisis simulation. Within minutes, they were talking over each other, missing details, and making conflicting decisions. I stopped the scenario and asked, "What do you actually know?"

Silence.

That's when it clicked.

"STOP" works because it restores clarity. It breaks panic loops. It turns noise into order.

At PCC Secure, it became our foundation for training security teams and executives alike. We teach it through real incidents, anthrax distribution drills, crowd control at major events, and dignitary protection logistics. The lesson is always the same: the first person to slow down usually becomes the leader, whether or not they hold the title.

The "STOP" Technique isn't complicated. It doesn't need a flowchart or software. It requires humility and the willingness to pause when everyone else is running.

Because leadership isn't about speed; it's about accuracy. And accuracy begins with stillness.

Leadership Principles:

- In a 2011 TED Talk, General Stanley McChrystal argued that leaders often fail not from lack of commitment, but from an inability to pause and reassess before acting.

- Stop the motion, Track the path, Observe the truth, Plan the fix. That's how you turn chaos into control.

- The next time everything feels urgent, remember, urgency is not an excuse for stupidity. It's an invitation to think.

CHAPTER 13
TRAIN UPWARD, NOT DOWNWARD

Every organization claims it wants leaders, but most only train followers.

Training downward means teaching people to execute tasks. Training upward means teaching them to understand and lead at the next level, or even two levels above their current position.

And that's the quiet failure behind every crisis I've ever worked on, the illusion of preparedness built on dependency. People are told precisely what to do but never taught how to think when the instructions stop working.

I first noticed it when I left government work and started consulting. In the NYPD and in OEM, we drilled often. We ran through scenarios, simulations, and tabletop exercises until they became muscle memory. You could drop most cops into a crisis, and they'd find a way to function. The system wasn't perfect, but the mindset was survival-driven. In the police department, if you wanted to get promoted to higher ranks, you had to study the Patrol

Guide, which delineated what each rank had to do in each situation. If you were a Police Officer and wanted to be a Sergeant, you studied for a big test on everything a Sergeant had to know and what to do in a given situation. The same held for Lieutenant and Captain. For each rank, you studied and learned what they did before you got promoted. If you passed and scored high enough, you got promoted.

Corporate America was different. They train downward, teaching the staff to execute, not to decide. Train them to perform tasks, not to understand context. Managers control information like currency, and subordinates are expected to operate blindly.

That difference hit me hard during a private-sector emergency management seminar. A room full of executives was discussing contingency planning. I asked, "If you went down tomorrow, who could take your place?"

Silence.

Finally, one of them laughed and said, "No one. That's why they pay me." His ego made him larger than life. He was "the man," the one who would lead through any crisis.

That single statement revealed everything wrong with American succession planning. He confused being needed with being effective. The most valuable leaders make themselves replaceable.

But did he have the ability to lead? This ego-driven illusion of indispensability puts companies at enormous risk. Leadership shifts into a bottleneck instead of being a shared asset.

Earlier, we saw the practice of holding classified or sensitive information close to oneself as a way to keep others from being as smart as you. This goes one step further. It's the question of relevance on a grand scale.

Corporate boards discuss succession planning and "key man" insurance. They hold the Chief Executive Officer accountable and ask, "Do you have a succession plan?" What they are really asking is, "If anything bad happens, are we covered?" The answer is always "of course we are," but the reality is rarely so.

That's the problem. Most organizations design themselves around the fragility of their leaders. They build hierarchies in which value derives from being irreplaceable rather than from effectiveness. It's an ego-driven model that collapses under pressure.

Corporate structures reward the illusion of control. You can see it in minor things: how managers hoard information, how departments guard budgets, how supervisors treat cross-training as a threat rather than an asset. Everyone protects their own relevance.

Succession planning in America is often little more than a checkbox on a corporate to-do list, rather than a robust strategy for organizational resilience. Most companies claim they value leadership development, yet fail to prepare the people beneath top executives to actually lead. The focus remains on immediate performance, training employees to complete tasks rather than to think critically or make decisions when circumstances deviate from the script. This gap creates an invisible but devastating fragility within organizations. When a leader is suddenly unavailable, the system grinds to a halt because no one else is ready to step up.

This failure isn't accidental. It showcases a deep-rooted mindset that prioritizes control and centralization over adaptability and empowerment. Lower-level managers and staff are rarely exposed to the broader context or taught to anticipate challenges beyond their assigned roles. Instead, they become experts at following orders rather than leading through a crisis. As a result, succession plans often sound good on paper but fall apart in practice because the people identified as "next in line" haven't been tested or nurtured to handle leadership in a crisis.

Contrast that with more resilient organizations, such as certain branches of the military, where succession is built into the culture. There, the norm is for each member to understand not only their job but also the jobs of their superiors, sometimes two or three levels above them. The logic is uncompromising: if one link in the chain breaks, the mission must continue. Training upward is not a luxury; it's a survival imperative. This mindset produces teams where taking initiative, stepping into new roles, and maintaining momentum under pressure are expected rather than exceptional.

Unfortunately, most American organizations perpetuate a culture of siloed knowledge and guarded authority. Information is treated as power to be hoarded rather than shared. Cross-training is seen as a threat rather than a safeguard. Rigid hierarchies and territorial attitudes stymie internal mobility. The result is a fragile system that cannot sustain itself when inevitable disruption occurs. Without genuine succession planning and investment in developing lower-level leaders, companies risk succumbing to chaos the moment leadership is tested or abruptly removed. The false comfort of "irreplaceable" leaders blinds us to the real cost of unpreparedness.

One thing I have noticed is how organizations delude themselves into thinking they are making great strides in developing new leaders by paying for additional college education, such as MBAs and specialized training programs. While these programs are excellent, and one can never overstate the benefits of education, their application in the home office is another matter. This raises the distinction between what I call practical and theoretical leadership. Providing advanced education to an individual should benefit all parties involved. The "student" receives education that can be applied within the corporation. The company benefits from using that education to its fullest. We have seen this termed as "an investment in the company's future."

That is theoretical leadership. It's what press releases are made of. It's what makes everyone feel excellent about themselves.

In most cases, practical leadership takes a bow for providing training, especially for underprivileged individuals it has taken under its wing, and rarely, if ever, uses it to its advantage. This creates frustration in the individual who has learned to perform tasks effectively through advanced training but is being stymied by leadership. The last thing an executive wants is an individual who has more training, is smarter, faster, and better-looking than they are.

As we see, leadership development is complex. Multiple factors are at play. The leader's ego leads them to believe they are indispensable. There is the belief that if they hold information no one else has, they are more intelligent than others and can be the only one to lead.

And then there is the embarrassment factor. Embarrassment arises when a person is publicly tested and shown not to have the answers they believed they had. This is best exemplified in facilitated discussions, which are a smaller, quicker form of tabletop exercise. It is a tool I often use with executive leadership that focuses narrowly on one topic, allowing no deviation. I run it for approximately one hour to accommodate executive schedules, sometimes even as a "lunch and learn." It provides a crisis topic with a slight touch of urgency to respond. It is almost impossible to recreate the actual tension in the room in a real crisis, but it can become interesting as participants sometimes get lost in the exercise.

I believe facilitated discussions are a cornerstone of effective crisis planning. They create a structured environment where leaders and teams can explore potential scenarios, identify gaps, and collaboratively develop response strategies. However, these conversations can also expose uncomfortable truths, especially when leaders come unprepared or lack the hands-on experience necessary to engage deeply. In such moments, facilitated discussions risk becoming arenas of embarrassment rather than of empowerment, revealing leaders' vulnerabilities to colleagues and stakeholders.

One of the biggest challenges is that many leaders don't have the bandwidth to immerse themselves fully in lengthy or complex planning exercises. Their schedules are packed with meetings, decisions, and daily operational demands, leaving them with scarce time, often no more than an hour, to devote to crisis planning. This constraint means that facilitated discussions must be sharply focused yet sufficiently dynamic to engage busy executives and simulate the stressful conditions of a crisis within an abbreviated timeframe. Striking this balance is difficult but essential.

When leaders aren't accustomed to crisis scenarios, even the thought of role-playing or walking through what-if situations can be intimidating. Without prior experience, they may hesitate to voice opinions or make rapid decisions under pressure during simulations, thereby highlighting gaps in preparedness and decision-making skills. This lack of confidence often becomes evident during facilitated discussions, subtly or sometimes overtly, undermining their authority and leaving them feeling exposed. The embarrassment stems not just from what they don't know, but also from the sudden, public nature of the readiness gap.

To counteract this, I try to design simulations that create a visceral sense of urgency without overwhelming participants. The goal is to replicate the stress and unpredictability of a crisis in a controlled setting that encourages authentic reactions and problem-solving. Engaging storytelling, realistic information injections, and time-sensitive decision points can foster the emotional and cognitive load leaders would feel in an actual emergency. This approach helps them understand what it feels like to be "in the hot seat" and reveals the pressures that real crises impose, not in a way that humiliates, but that informs and motivates.

As I develop the scenarios, I must ensure that I include measures to foster psychological safety, so that leaders feel supported rather than judged. Emphasizing that the purpose is growth, not blame, can help diminish defensiveness. Setting expectations up front about the exercises and explaining that feeling uncomfortable is part of the learning process creates space for openness. When leaders trust that the environment is constructive, they are more likely to engage fully, revealing gaps that might otherwise stay hidden until a real crisis strikes.

Ultimately, facilitated discussions in crisis planning must balance realism with empathy and time constraints with depth. Even in a one-hour session, it's possible to catalyze a meaningful experience that shakes leaders out of complacency and exposes the urgency of preparedness. The key lies in thoughtful design and skilled facilitation that draw out authentic reactions, encourage reflection, and lay the groundwork for ongoing development, turning potential embarrassment into a powerful catalyst for leadership growth.

Training upward isn't about hierarchy; it's about continuity. It's preparing people to lead when no one is watching. It's building a culture where the question "who's in charge?" doesn't matter because everyone understands the mission.

When I ask companies today how they train, they describe certifications, compliance, and checklists.

I ask again, "Who are you developing to replace you?"

They laugh, uncomfortable. Most leaders can't imagine grooming their successors because they view leadership as possession rather than stewardship.

But the truth is simple: if your team can't function without you, you haven't led, you've hoarded.

That's what the Marines understand, and what too many civilian organizations forget. Leadership isn't what you build above you. It's what you leave behind.

In every organization that fails under pressure, the root cause is the same: no one knows what to do once the leader leaves the room.

That's not a personnel problem; it's a leadership design flaw.

The difference between upward and downward training often determines whether a team adapts under pressure or collapses into chaos. Training that flows only downward emphasizes compliance and repetition, producing obedience but little judgment. Training that moves upward encourages initiative, learning, independent thinking, and adaptability rather than reliance. Over time, the former creates dependency, while the latter develops depth. In complex environments, survival depends far more on the latter.

The Marines understood this long before most modern leaders did. Their leadership philosophy isn't theoretical; it's practical. They train their people to think, decide, and act as leaders long before they carry the title. It's not about ambition; it's about survival.

These principles are timeless because they're built on human behavior rather than bureaucracy. They assume chaos. They assume imperfection. They teach leaders to plan for the moment when everything stops functioning.

When I translate these ideas for corporate clients, I replace the military terms "command" and "team" with "mission" and "project." The core doesn't change. Whether you're running a Marine squad or a major company, the questions are identical: Do your people know the plan? Can they execute it without you? Will they hold the line when things fall apart?

Upward training answers yes to all three.

In the private sector, it's easy to hide behind structure, titles, metrics, policies, and risk assessments. Those things create the illusion of control, but none of them can think. Only people can. "The measure of a leader isn't how many people depend on them; it's how many people don't need to," is a quote featured in James Kerr's book Legacy: *What the All Blacks Can Teach Us About the Business of Life*, which examines the principles of success and leadership demonstrated by the New Zealand national rugby team, the *All Blacks*. The central theme emphasizes that a true and lasting legacy is measured by enduring influence and positive impact on future generations, rather than by temporary control or material achievements.

That's how you build organizational immunity. You assume loss and design continuity.

Training upward requires humility. It means teaching people to be as good as you or better. It means accepting that your legacy will be measured not by what you controlled but by what endures.

That's the lesson most executives never learn. They're so focused on maintaining authority that they forget the point of leadership is to make yourself obsolete. If your team can thrive without you, you've done your job.

That corporate executive who believed no one could replace him was wrong. The question isn't whether someone can replace you; it's whether you prepared them to. That's the difference between training downward and training upward. One protects your ego, the other protects the mission.

Because leadership isn't about permanence, it's about transfer. The best leaders don't build followers. They build replacements.

....

Leadership Principles:

- Downward training protects the ego, while upward training protects the mission.

- If your organization can't function without your presence, you haven't built a team; you've built a dependency. Authentic leadership isn't measured by control; it's measured by continuity. Train people to lead when you're gone. That's how you create stability through chaos.

PART 4
LEADING
IN PUBLIC

CHAPTER 14
PUBLIC VERSUS PRIVATE LEADERSHIP FAILURES

People love to compare government and business. They think one's bloated and bureaucratic, the other sleek and efficient. But after decades working in both, I can tell you the truth: they're twins, dressed differently, speaking different languages, but driven by the same instincts.

The only real difference is what they're afraid of.

In government, leaders fear embarrassment and potential political suicide. Let's be honest. Political leadership, regardless of the party you support, is a mess. The old Superman saying of "truth, justice, and the American way" is long gone. What might once have been considered an honest profession, although I seriously doubt that, is now an open invitation for corruption and personal advancement. How can an elected official, who has never held a real job leading others or running a successful company, earn a mere $180,000 a year and amass a fortune of millions in such a short time? Today, political leaders lack a moral compass. They are in it for their own greedy benefit. They have little to no leadership experience, yet they are the ones we turn to when a crisis hits. They surround themselves with flunkies, who have even less of an idea than they do, telling them that they are wonderful and insightful. Remember the FEMA flunky who wanted to measure the Mayor's desk? And we wonder why things are so screwed up?

Politicians love to come up with the big idea, the concept that will solve the world's problems. What they never understand or pay any attention to is the law of "unintended consequences." A press release or a soundbite for television is sufficient. Crises don't happen in a vacuum. They are long and drawn-out affairs, but the kiddies around the politicians think they can solve the problems quickly. The politician gets the sound bite and appears to be a hero. It is a win-win situation for everyone involved except the public.

Over the years, as I have shown, I have been both fortunate and unfortunate enough to be part of events that continue to confirm my beliefs. As I said in an earlier chapter, we are safe despite ourselves, but that theory is becoming increasingly difficult to believe every day. Leadership decisions often make me want to scratch my head and say, WTF? Here are two excellent examples.

Upon my retirement from the NYPD, I was certified as a "Technical Assistant Provider" by the U.S. Department of Justice. In this role, I conducted assessments for states applying for federal grant funding to combat terrorism. This wasn't a full-time role; it was a contractor position with a vendor handling tasks assigned by the DOJ. Most of the time, I was asked to assist with assessments; at other times, I served as the "law enforcement controller" in terrorism exercises ranging from the Olympics to local exercises.

One such exercise was to test the distribution of the "National Push Package."

The National Push Package was a concept that made perfect sense, on paper, until the law of unintended consequences reared its ugly head. Let me explain.

In 1999, following Congressional direction, the U.S. established the concept of "push packages" known as the National Pharmaceutical Stockpile (NPS) to prepackage medical supplies for rapid deployment during large-scale emergencies. The first "push-package" formulary was developed that year. This evolved into the Strategic National Stockpile (SNS) in 2003. Crates of medical supplies were packaged and ready to be deployed into Cities that were suffering from an actual terrorism event. The stockpiling of medications, like antibiotics, for use in a biological attack, ventilators, and other first aid materials were all part of the package.

I was asked to travel to Denver to serve as a law-enforcement controller and to test the distribution process. There were security issues that required testing. We needed to assess the risks of transporting the "push packages" to airports, then break them down for further distribution, all while considering security implications and determining the best way to deliver the material to the locations where it was needed without being compromised, stolen, or worse. The fear was that the packages could be intercepted and stolen at any given point. The entire "point of distribution" needed to be analyzed and tested.

The delivery of NPS components to Denver was largely notional, but material resembling the components of an actual package was flown in. There were people responsible for every step of the exercise. Once the package "safely" arrived, it was taken into a hangar for disassembly. A woman was responsible for taking the simulated "anti-biotics" and further breaking them down. What she was faced with were large boxes filled with M&M's. Loose, dumped in a box. Someone thought that was a great idea. Put thousands of M&M's in boxes, loose, and expect an effective, timely distribution of "anti-biotics." That was the first problem. As they say on TV, but wait, there's more.

The next problem came when she was required to break the M&M's down into doses. There were no pill counters in the package. She had a box on the table, and decided to start counting, but there was a bigger problem. She had nowhere to put them. Frantic calls were being made between the site and the controllers back in Washington, D.C. So, what did our fearless leaders come up with? Let us send someone to the local Safeway supermarket to buy plastic bags. That someone was me. The law of unintended consequences struck again.

The next situation worth mentioning was the government's discussion and direction on the use of plastic wrap and duct tape to seal homes in the event of a chemical attack.

It was so well thought out that the government website, www.ready.gov/hazmat, recommends it as a tactic to use to stay safe from a chemical attack. Multiple news stations asked me to give an interview about the effectiveness of plastic and duct tape. It was hard to keep a straight face during the interviews. In one, we interviewed at Home Depot, in front of the duct tape aisle. I couldn't get the cartoon to stop running in my head with the character who wrapped plastic around his home, duct taped it, and stood there, proud of himself. That was until he had an "Urkel" moment. Urkel was a character from the TV show "Family Matters" who would do things that went wrong, then look around and say in that distinctive voice, "Did I do that?" It was then that the guy started to wonder how he was supposed to get into the home after it was sealed.

Yet we need to remember that we are safe despite ourselves.

The duct tape guidance perfectly illustrates how government leadership fails: someone issued a recommendation without considering the second-order effects: the consequences of consequences, the ripple effects most leaders never consider. It looked good on paper. It was useless in practice. And it eroded public trust in actual emergency preparedness.

These government failures taught me something important: the public sector doesn't have a monopoly on incompetence. When I moved into the private sector, I discovered the same patterns, just wearing different clothes.

In business, they fear loss. But both public and private lead defensively.

I learned that the first time I left a government office for a corporate boardroom. I'd spent years fighting through layers of red tape, turf wars, and endless "confidential" meetings. I thought moving into the private sector would be liberating, a place where decisions were faster, authority was more apparent, and competence actually mattered.

It didn't take long to realize I was wrong.

Shortly after I retired from the NYPD, I founded Protective Consultants, a company that provided security consulting services primarily to commercial real estate corporations. It was a natural fit and leveraged the title I had received in OEM: Director of Security and Intelligence Operations. I had been working for the Mayor of New York, Rudy Giuliani, back when he was considered America's Mayor. I had "contacts" from around the world that I could turn to for both business and as resources. I had decided to retire from the department near the end of January 2001. On New Year's Eve, the Mayor visited the command center, where a significant operation was underway. As he left, I took the elevator with him to the street and mentioned that I would be retiring. He was gracious, thanked me for my service, and offered to help if I needed anything. I had spent his first term conducting threat assessments and investigations, conducting significant event site assessments, and handling other security matters for him and other elected officials. There were many nights I had to go to Gracie Mansion, the Mayoral residence, to brief him on threats. We definitely knew each other.

While many on the protective detail chose to remain with him after he left office, I decided that, given the benefits available to me, I would do it alone. Protective Consultants started with a "bang" and grew quickly. It wasn't long before a colleague, Jim Henry, whom I met through a mutual client, Silverstein Properties, became a close working friend. Jim was a legend in the security world. He was the co-owner of Henry Brothers, a security integration company, founded by his father and uncles.

Just after 9/11, Henry Brothers went public as Diversified Security. Jim was the Chairman of the Board and Chief Executive Officer. Shortly thereafter, they initiated a major merger-and-acquisition program. Under pressure from the company that had taken them public to establish a consulting division, he approached me with an offer to acquire Protective Consultants. As part of the agreement, I was appointed President of the consulting division, Executive Vice President of the company, and a member of the Board of Directors. We were traded on the American Stock Exchange under the symbol DVS.

The experience of serving on a public board provided lessons that no business graduate program could offer. It also required me to learn fast and use all the training I had received from the Hostage Negotiation Team. It was during these meetings that I realized how important the stock price was and the effects our actions would have on it. At this level, the business became less about generating sales and more about managing investors. As the number three man in the operation, I had to spend time with the attorneys to understand what could and could not be said in public comments, and with the press relations team for the same reason.

The pressures I faced on that board revealed a truth: private sector leaders face the same fear-based decision-making as politicians; they're just afraid of different consequences. Politicians fear voters; executives fear shareholders. Both lead defensively.

During internal meetings, I learned a valuable lesson. Never want something so bad that you are willing to consider bending your moral values. Some in leadership positions believed the stock price could be managed. If you had a million shares and it went up a dollar, you just made a million dollars. If it went down, you lost a million. All of this was hypothetical; however, for someone thinking in this way, greed would take over, especially if they were close to retirement.

I was very cautious. I left law enforcement with an "if you do that, you go to jail" mentality. Others in the company were willing to push the envelope to the limit, and perhaps even cross it a bit. I, on the other hand, was the "bull in the China shop." That attitude definitely caused some friction. I guess you really shouldn't ask the President, "How fucking stupid are you in a meeting?

Poor Jim was always caught in the middle of the fights. He would never cross the line and always knew how to listen to ideas and concepts and then make the right decision. I learned a great deal from him, both in the technical aspects of security and in how to deal at a corporate level with people whose abilities may not be at the level one would expect. He had considerable patience, which I clearly lack. This year, we lost Jim to pancreatic cancer. I hope he knows how much he is missed.

Over the years, the issues corporations face today remain the same as they were then. Despite every effort to advance capabilities and effectiveness, progress is hindered by entrenched thinking. In every crisis I get called into, it always comes down to the same few things. Boards want a security plan, but do not want to hear about the associated liabilities, and executives who want to be the smartest person in the room. It always fascinates me when a client calls for help, then completely discounts what you tell them because they know better. I firmly believe in letting the adults do their jobs. I wouldn't tell a neurosurgeon how to operate on the brain. Let the experts determine the path, or at least consider the options they provide. Many executives think they know better.

By not being a yes-man, I have lost clients, but I have always believed in looking out for the client, even when the client acts against their own interests. I never want a client to think I have my hand in their pocket, that I am just there to make money. Sometimes caring costs money.

Just before writing this book, I experienced such an episode. It was a private company, but a significant investment holding company held most of the shares. It was a mom-and-pop operation, but it played at a very high level, both nationally and internationally. I was contracted to provide security consulting services on several physical security issues. During this time, a crisis developed that they were totally unprepared for.

An employee had become dissatisfied at work to the point that he became increasingly vocal with his displeasure with leadership. One day, annoyed by an insignificant act, such as a door opening, he issued a threat. What he said was, "I should go home and get my gun and come back and kill them!" He wasn't quiet about it; people around him heard him. The staff who heard it went to the HR department. HR went to leadership, and what did they do? They called a meeting to discuss. It took a couple of days before they could get an answer and a sense of direction. Leadership buried its head in the sand, and made the same statements, albeit excuses, we are all too familiar with: "He really isn't that kind of guy, I don't think he is serious."

The resulting delay caused more problems. Word of the threat spread quickly throughout the organization. Staff refused to come to the office. Leadership brought in an armed guard during working hours to alleviate fears. They received a guard who was very tall, dressed in black, wearing a bulletproof vest, a gun belt ready for war, and tactical pants and boots. The only thing missing was the bandolier draped across his chest like Poncho Villa. All at the leadership's direction.

Eventually, the employee was sent home and later terminated. What is interesting, and we see this in many places, is the lack of understanding of what can happen in what appears to be a split second. How many times must we read about a workplace violence shooting and hear about the red flags that were missed? When the investigation comes after the shooting, it is not uncommon to hear that leadership knew and did nothing. How uncomfortable can it be to sit in front of a microphone and be asked the great question: what did you know, and when did you know it?

This is the essence of private leadership failure made painfully public: leaders so insulated in their own judgment that they dismiss clear warning signs while those in their charge fear for their lives. The subsequent appearance of a paramilitary-style security guard, complete with tactical gear and visible weaponry, only amplified the terror they had initially downplayed. What should have taken minutes to address, immediate removal of the threatening employee, and consultation with threat assessment professionals, instead stretched into days of organizational paralysis. The leadership's arrogance created the very crisis they thought they were preventing, transforming a manageable situation into widespread panic that emptied their offices.

This failure exemplifies why organizations cannot afford to leave threat assessments to untrained administrators who believe good intentions substitute for expertise. The red flags in this case weren't subtle; they were screaming alarms that leadership chose to ignore because acknowledging them would require uncomfortable, immediate action.

We have a program, the Threat Assessment Group (TAG), explicitly designed for this type of situation. It examines the problem of workplace violence from the outset, when it is often dismissed, and tracks the inappropriate correspondence, statements, and behaviors before they become violent. Trying to solve the problem after the fact is like trying to catch lightning in a bottle. It can't easily be done. Yet most leadership today fails to prevent such events. It is probably one of the worst failures we continue to face.

In government, the enemy of progress is politics. Every decision passes through a filter of "How will this play?" before anyone asks, "Will this work?" Accountability exists, but it's distant, spread across committees, agencies, and review boards. Responsibility is diluted until no one can be held accountable.

When I left OEM and started consulting, I realized private clients were craving what the government once gave me: rules. They want clarity and structure. But when those same systems demanded transparency, they recoiled. They want order without scrutiny.

It always comes down to the same human flaw: people want authority without vulnerability.

That's why both systems build echo chambers. They reward people who tell them what they want to hear. In government, it's policy advisors and staffers who translate uncertainty into sound bites. In business, it's consultants and analysts who translate risk into "strategic optimism." Both trade honesty for approval, and approval is money.

And when a crisis hits, it all falls apart like a deck of cards.

I've watched boards of directors and emergency committees make the same fatal mistake, confusing the ability to communicate with the ability to lead.

Communication doesn't save you. Action does, but fear can be paralyzing.

But here's the hard truth: both systems are capable of brilliance when led by people who understand this. The key difference between dysfunction and effectiveness isn't about having more resources; it's about adopting the right mindset to utilize the resources you have.

That's why *Leading Through Chaos* isn't a book about agencies or industries; it's a book about behavior.

Behavior determines whether a government official hides behind a committee or a CEO behind a slogan. Behavior decides whether teams adapt or collapse. Systems don't lead, people do, and their behavior is the difference.

When I work with executives in one-on-one sessions now, I ask them: "If your title disappeared tomorrow, what value would you still bring?" It is a brutal question that strips away illusion. Those who answer confidently and can explain their process, not just their position, are the real leaders. The fakes disappear when the camera turns off.

Drawing on ideas popularized by author and management expert Simon Sinek, leadership transcends sector, hierarchy, and title, placing greater weight on clarity, courage, and humility than on formal authority.

If you want to see authentic leadership, look for the person who's willing to say, "I don't know yet, but I'll find out." You'll find them in both worlds, often buried under layers of people talking louder.

Leadership Principles:

- Titles, budgets, and systems don't fail. People do. And they fail for human reasons, ego, fear, and silence.

- Drawing on leadership principles articulated by Colin Powell, effective leadership succeeds when accountability is personal and communication is honest, regardless of sector or rank.

CHAPTER 15
THE PRESS, SOCIAL MEDIA, AND THE 24 HOUR RULE

Today's leaders don't fail because of what goes wrong. They fail because of how they respond, and in the age of social media, that response is instant, permanent, and unforgiving.

The press operates on its own timeline and agenda, demanding immediate responses and often amplifying every misstep. When leaders fail to manage media relations effectively, confusion and misinformation can spread rapidly, exacerbating the crisis itself.

This is a modern reality that did not exist when many current leaders were trained. Incidents are inevitable, systems fail, and people will make mistakes. Weather, chance, and bad luck all play a role. What has changed is that responses now unfold publicly, in real time, under emotional pressure, with no natural pause built into the process. As I said before, the news cycle has shifted from three days to immediate.

Here's what most leaders still don't understand: social media isn't different from traditional media. It IS media: without editors, without delay, and without mercy.

I know recognition is changing, especially given its impact in the 2024 elections. Still, for many leaders, it's not the same as traditional media outlets such as CNN or Fox News. That lack of understanding of what it truly is and how deadly it can be to a career cannot be overstated.

In earlier eras, leaders had time, sometimes hours, sometimes days, to understand what happened, gather facts, consult advisors, and craft a response that reflected the organization rather than the individual. Today, leaders are expected to respond immediately, often before they fully understand the issue. Silence is interpreted as a sign of weakness and as a questioning of the leader's capabilities. Delay is viewed as guilt. It is considered hiding and seeking a good excuse before going public with any statements. Restraint is misread as uncertainty and as a lack of effectiveness.

In addition, social media's 24/7 nature means crises never truly "stop," placing relentless pressure on leaders to respond continuously and adapt messaging in real time. This constant flow of information saturates both leadership and the public, often resulting in message fatigue or confusion. Social media also enables direct, unfiltered communication from leaders, which can be a double-edged sword. While platforms offer a chance to connect swiftly with the public, any misstatement is instantly recorded, shared, and dissected. Misinformation is generated from misstatements made by leadership and also by those who think, either because of a cognitive bias or a bad sense of humor, that putting out what is to be considered facts amounts to nothing more than a bad joke.

A poignant example is the spread of misinformation during the COVID-19 pandemic, when social platforms were flooded with unproven cures and conspiracy theories, complicating public health communication efforts. Self-appointed "experts" with no medical training or scientific credentials commanded massive online audiences, confidently prescribing everything from bleach ingestion to livestock deworming medications as COVID treatments. These individuals, lifestyle influencers, political commentators, and conspiracy theorists, spoke with an authority they hadn't earned, yet their messages spread faster and reached further than guidance from actual epidemiologists and infectious disease specialists. People who wouldn't trust an unlicensed plumber to fix their pipes were suddenly taking medical advice from podcasters and social media personalities whose only qualification was a large following and a confident delivery.

The platforms themselves amplified this dangerous noise. Algorithms designed to maximize engagement elevated sensational misinformation over careful scientific explanations, because outrage and fear drive more clicks than measured public health guidance. A doctor with thirty years of experience in infectious disease could post a nuanced explanation of how vaccines work, reaching perhaps a few thousand people. Meanwhile, a fitness influencer's video claiming that vitamins and "natural immunity" were all anyone needed could go viral, reaching millions within hours. The asymmetry was staggering: lies traveled at the speed of shares and retweets, while truth moved at the cautious pace of peer review and clinical trials.

In some cases, these false narratives have led to real-world consequences, including vaccine hesitancy and public distrust of health authorities. Families refused proven treatments for loved ones gasping for air in ICU beds. Emergency rooms saw poisonings from people self-administering industrial chemicals they'd seen promoted online. Vaccination rates plummeted in communities where misinformation took hold, leading to preventable deaths and prolonged outbreaks. Perhaps most insidiously, the constant barrage of false information eroded trust in the very institutions, the CDC, WHO, and medical establishment, that possessed actual expertise. When everyone with a smartphone could claim to be an authority, actual authority became just another opinion to be dismissed. This wasn't merely a failure of communication; it was a public health crisis, amplified by a complete breakdown in society's ability to distinguish between credible expertise and confident ignorance.

The age-old adage that "there is no such thing as bad press" no longer exists. Your credibility is what you can control. How you position yourself in the public eye matters in your professional life. Some get caught up in the limited public recognition they receive from TV appearances. You have to control your ego when it comes to TV. I always try to live by the simple rule, "never believe in your own headlines."

When speaking publicly, especially in live environments, the goal should not be to command attention. It is to provide clarity without creating fear or worse, making you the target. Sometimes the press pushes for the dramatic because it makes great TV; other times, we create the drama.

My media experiences repeatedly reinforced this lesson. I learned that credibility isn't built through dramatic language or alarming statements. It's built through consistency, restraint, and accuracy; otherwise, you become that "cartoon" character they bring on air for comic relief. You shouldn't have a "shtick" as a professional leader; leave that to the actors and comedians. Once, I was replaced on a TV news set. The producers cut to a quick commercial, and a new "guest" was brought on because I wouldn't get excited about the news channel's coverage. I wasn't there for dramatic effect; I was there as the expert. The situation they were covering was a routine rescue. No danger to the people involved, no reason to have people sitting on the edge of their seats. It must have been a slow news day. The person who followed me turned it into exactly what the TV station wanted, a life and death drama. Unfortunately for them, the person being rescued opened his lunch box, took out a sandwich, and started eating while the Fire Department went about the rescue. Nothing like high afternoon drama!

Over the years, we have seen how one statement can turn an entire event from chaotic to pure chaos. Here is one great example.

During the 2010 BP Deepwater Horizon oil spill, the CEO, Tony Hayward, faced intense media scrutiny after making the infamous comment, "I want my life back," in a press interview. This sparked public outrage and became a symbol of corporate insensitivity. This example illustrates how mishandling press interactions can increase public distrust and, more importantly, escalate chaos.

The emotional toll on leaders during high-pressure crises such as the 2010 BP Deepwater Horizon oil spill cannot be overstated. Tony Hayward, as CEO, faced immense stress, relentless media scrutiny, urgent demands for answers, and the weight of corporate responsibility amid a human and environmental disaster. In such an emotionally charged atmosphere, even offhand remarks can carry disproportionate consequences. His comment, "I want my life back," reflected a moment of personal exhaustion and frustration, yet it was broadcast publicly without context. This exposes the vulnerability leaders face as they navigate the emotional strain of crisis management under the unforgiving media spotlight. No one wants to stop and consider the context of what is being said; they merely look at the content and run with it.

Press statements made during crises are often dissected, quoted out of context, or framed in ways that amplify negative interpretations consistent with the person's or the press's agenda at the time. What may be intended as a candid human moment can be perceived by the public as callous or indifferent. In Hayward's case, the phrase "I want my life back" was widely interpreted as insensitive to the environmental devastation and human suffering caused by the spill. The backlash transformed a private expression of fatigue into a public symbol of corporate disregard. This misinterpretation highlights the critical challenge leaders face: the need to communicate clearly, with empathy, and with an acute awareness of how words can be received and reframed by both the press and the public. Under these rules of engagement, it is a wonder how any statements are made publicly anymore.

Furthermore, the fallout from such problematic press interactions extends well beyond immediate reputational damage. Hayward's statement not only intensified public outrage but also complicated BP's ongoing response efforts, creating additional hurdles in rebuilding trust with stakeholders and the community. The company incurred significant financial losses and sustained lasting damage to its brand integrity. This example demonstrates how a single ill-considered press comment can escalate chaos by undermining a leader's credibility and diverting attention from the substantive crisis response. It underscores the necessity for leaders to prepare meticulously for media engagements, balancing authenticity with strategic communication to manage both the factual and emotional dimensions of a crisis.

Is it fair to hold someone to that standard? We have all said things in the heat of a discussion that we wish we could have taken back. Very few of us want to be quoted word-for-word for what we say. A little bit of fear or apprehension before an interview always helps me think through what I am going to say. Sometimes it actually works.

When it comes to interviews, I much prefer live interviews to recorded ones. In a live interview, what you said is what you said. The average interview lasts about three minutes, with the average number of questions being about two to three, depending on the length of your answer. The reporters don't have time to go back and change what you said in the moment. Sure, we have seen reports and court cases about politicians claiming their interviews were edited inaccurately, but for the most part, they are stuck with live interviews. When they record the interview, they have greater latitude to manipulate what you said, using your own words and a little creative "B" roll footage.

This happened to me during an interview about the rebuilding of the World Trade Center, where a New York reporter manipulated the interview to advance her preferred narrative and support her story.

To begin with, I know many people in the news business: some are reporters, some are producers, and some are in production. Except for a very few, I respect most of them for their abilities and dedication. There are, though, a few, and one in particular, that I have no respect for.

As the story goes, architectural drawings were found in a dumpster near the construction site of the Freedom Tower. The person who found it reported it, and the media obtained it. The reporter was determined to write a story about the security implications of carelessly discarding such documents in the trash. A producer I had worked with previously called and asked whether I could meet the reporter at the site to be interviewed about the plans. During the interview, it became clear that the plans she had were not construction plans but a rental plan showing floor layouts. No critical infrastructure was shown on the plans, no electrical connections, no gas lines, nothing but wide open floor spaces. But the story she wanted was the possibility that a terrorist organization like Al Qaeda or ISIS could get their hands on the plans and commit another 9/11 attack. That couldn't be farther from the truth, but not to her.

During the interview, she directed her cameraman to film her and me as we went over the plans. I was pointing out that it was useless for planning a terrorist attack. What she said was about how it could be used.

Those who saw the interview knew me better and knew I wouldn't say what she alluded to. I still had to explain to some that it was all theater on her part. To this day, I refuse to interview with her.

Fortunately, the story faded away quickly. Those who know, know the press and the sensationalism they desire. There was no outcry on social media. Even the lunatics who jump on everything didn't bite. I was fortunate, but there are other cases where people are less fortunate, especially when it comes to social media and how leadership gets drawn into the fray.

This experience taught me two lessons: First, recorded interviews give journalists editorial control you can never get back. Second, always assume your words will be used in the worst possible context.

The media's power to shape narratives is formidable, but it pales in comparison to the wild, ungoverned chaos of social media, where context dies instantly, and outrage spreads like wildfire. In traditional media, there's at least a gatekeeper, an editor, a producer, someone making decisions about what gets published. On social media platforms, there are no gatekeepers, only algorithms designed to amplify whatever generates the most emotional response. A single post, stripped of all context and nuance, can destroy a reputation in hours. What took the traditional press days or weeks to build into a story can now explode across millions of screens before anyone even knows what happened. And when leadership gets pulled into these digital firestorms, their response, or lack thereof, can determine whether the crisis burns out or consumes everything in its path. The following case illustrates how quickly a private moment can become a very public leadership crisis, and how the decisions made in those first critical hours can mean the difference between containment and catastrophe.

I received an urgent call from a client facing a developing crisis regarding an eleven-second video on social media.

His son was away at college, and he and his girlfriend were having a date night. In the late evening, they were lying around, and the girlfriend took an eleven-second video of him rambling, no context for what he was saying, just content. Nothing made any sense, just rambling words, and the use of the N word. She intended to send the video to her girlfriend on a social media platform. What she did was post it for all to see at approximately 11 pm. Within minutes, it spread rapidly, and thousands saw it. By 8 am, over 100,000 people had viewed it. By 3 pm, over two hundred thousand, and then the death threats started to come. By that evening, the family's home address was public.

Where the case takes a turn is the way the parents get involved. The family had taken a Christmas picture in front of the fireplace at their home. It was posted on social media, and when it was examined, the coordinates where it was taken popped up. The protestors now knew where the family lived and threatened to come to the home to "teach them a lesson."

Once that information was out, the next step was for the protesters to target the father's business. He ran a significant financial services business, and the potential impact was substantial.

Fortunately, the crisis ended without anyone being killed or injured. The lives of the entire family were upended for months, and the situation eventually subsided as the protestors moved on. The potential damage could have been devastating.

Sometimes, leadership faces a crisis it did not create and is drawn into. Other times, they are the reason.

I was asked to get involved in a case where a female corporate leader was having an affair with a married man. The affair went on for a long time, and during that period, they became "friendly" enough for him to take some explicit photos of her. They even had pet names for each other.

One day, the wife, suspicious, took the husband's phone and found the pictures. She also found the girlfriend's email address and an AOL account. Taking a shot at being a spy, she goes to AOL, types in the girlfriend's email address, and uses the pet name he had for her as the password. It actually worked. She then downloaded the pictures from her husband's phone into the girlfriend's AOL account and sent them to everyone in her directory. Multiple emails were sent with subject lines like, "What a wild weekend I just had."

To most people, the story is a little comical at this point, but it takes a turn for the worse when we learn that her email list includes her son's email address. He was a Marine stationed in Iraq. He received the emails that the wife sent through his mother's AOL account. The mother was devastated, noting that if he were distracted by the emails and were hurt or killed, she could never forgive herself.

Social media also creates vulnerabilities that extend beyond the leader. This is not about secrecy; it is about protection. Family members do not consent to exposure as leaders. They do not benefit from visibility or have control over the narrative. Bringing them onto public platforms introduces emotional variables that leaders cannot manage as pressure increases.

Another critical rule I always follow is to stay apolitical. Social media blurs professional authority with personal ideology; leaders who allow those lines to merge instantly and permanently lose credibility with half their audience. Once a leader is seen as aligned with a political identity online, every future decision is filtered through that lens.

This does not mean leaders lack opinions. It means they understand context. Public platforms are not private spaces. The most important insight from years of watching leadership failures play out publicly is this. They are judged by outsiders who do not know the whole story and never will. That reality cannot be changed; the perception must be managed.

Social media did not create leadership failure. It revealed how many leaders mistake speed for strength and visibility for control.

The leaders who adapt understand that public communication is now a core leadership function. They train for it. They practice discipline. They build rules into their behavior before crises occur, not after.

A part of this discipline is practicing the 24-hour rule for email. For starters, studies show that leaders should check email only three to four times a day; otherwise, they become reactive rather than strategic. How many hours are lost answering emails or worse, text messages that a two-minute phone call can answer? We have become like Pavlov's dogs: when the phone dings, we pick it up, only to be drawn into a conversation that goes on forever. However, most of these interruptions are not inherently dangerous. But emails and texts can quickly escalate to a crisis when you apply an emotional tag to them.

As we continuously see, the problem with today's communication methods is a lack of context for what is written. We understand content, but context is more difficult. How often have we gotten a text or email and wondered what the person was really trying to say? Worse, how many times have we reacted with emotion to the communication, only to later learn that our interpretation was totally different than the intent of what was sent?

In intelligence work, the distinction between content and context is often difficult to draw. The message's context can be the real threat. Systems are being developed using AI to close the gap and provide more accurate warnings when threats can be identified.

In today's business environment, we sometimes receive problematic emails or texts. We respond emotionally to correspondence, especially when it comes from someone we respect little or outright dislike. My first response is to write back, typically beginning with something like "Dear Douche Bag…" or a similar greeting. Obviously, this is the wrong approach, and I can't say I'm entirely innocent of using something very similar.

As I progressed in my career, I began using the 24-hour rule. There are variations of this rule, but I keep it simple. When I get a message that pisses me off, I hold back for at least 24 hours before I respond. What usually comes is something more professional, but stated, and still gets my point across.

As the U.S. Surgeon General Vivek Murthy observed, "Emotional responses feel authentic in the moment, but disciplined, delayed responses protect both credibility and institutional trust over time." The 24-hour rule operationalizes this wisdom.

As with the rest of the medical advice I receive, I should follow the doctor's advice. It has kept me out of trouble so far.

....

Leadership Principles:

- Leaders are no longer judged primarily by what goes wrong, but by how they respond under public pressure and compressed timelines.

- In a twenty-four-hour media environment, restraint is leadership.

CHAPTER 16
CLOSING LESSONS: WE ARE SAFE IN SPITE OF OURSELVES

A line has stayed with me longer than most lessons from my intelligence and crisis work. We are safe in spite of ourselves.

That statement is not cynical. It is descriptive.

The public often assumes safety exists because systems function as designed, leaders are competent, and institutions function smoothly. The reality is far less orderly. Safety exists because people within those systems care enough to compensate for flaws. People who stay late. People who double-check. People who warn even when they are ignored. People who quietly fix what should not have been broken in the first place.

That is why this book exists.

It was not intended to expose secrets or elevate individuals, nor was it designed to ridicule or criticize the system, except for those few Darwin Award winners who deserved special recognition. It is to make visible the reality that most organizations survive not because they are well-designed, but because they are continually accommodated by professionals who understand their weaknesses and work around them, individuals who outmaneuver leadership's incompetence.

Plans are adjusted. Procedures are bent. Gaps are bridged informally. Decisions are softened to avoid political consequences. Accountability is often deferred rather than enforced. In many environments, holding people accountable creates more friction than tolerating inefficiency, thereby normalizing inefficiency.

Every lesson I've learned, from the NYPD to OEM to the private sector, came from moments when the plan fell apart, and people sought direction. That's when leadership starts: when there's no script, no guarantee, and no one else willing to make the call. Titles mean nothing when there is incompetence. True leaders step up to the plate and take a swing.

For years, I thought chaos was the enemy. I fought it, contained it, tried to outthink it. But over time, I realized it was the teacher. Every failure, every argument, every sleepless night was a test, not of my knowledge, but of my composure.

Chaos exposes who you are when titles and systems collapse.

I've seen leadership under every kind of pressure, political, physical, and emotional. I've observed police officers command without authority because their tone was calm when others were shouting. I've seen CEOs with resources collapse because they couldn't admit fear. I've seen young analysts in windowless rooms make better decisions than the people running entire agencies, simply because they were willing to stop and think.

Leading through crisis doesn't care who you are, only how you act.

Over the decades, I've met people who confuse leadership with authority, or charisma, or intelligence. But chaos doesn't care about any of that. It only measures clarity and courage.

The clearest person in the room wins.

And that clarity doesn't come from certainty; it comes from discipline. The discipline to slow down, ask questions, listen longer, and decide when everyone else hesitates.

The best leaders I've known shared one thing in common: humility. They knew how little control they really had. They respected chaos instead of fearing it. They didn't waste energy trying to dominate every variable; they built teams and systems that could adapt to any variable.

That's why, in the end, *Leading through Chaos* isn't about strategy; it's about acceptance. You can't eliminate chaos, but you can learn its rhythm. You can move with it instead of against it.

Because the world won't wait for your plan, it will always outrun you.

The longer you lead, the more you understand that chaos isn't an interruption; it's the environment. The people who spend their lives trying to control it end up exhausted, cynical, and eventually broken.

Throughout my career, I watched people do the right thing quietly, often without recognition, and sometimes in direct opposition to leadership preferences. They were not reckless. They were responsible. They understood that waiting for permission can be more dangerous than acting with restraint. What's the saying, "it's better to beg for forgiveness than to ask for permission?"

That tension sits at the center of leadership.

All of this brings us to the practical reality that separates prepared leaders from those caught flat-footed when crisis strikes. Understanding second-order effects, avoiding perverse incentives, and maintaining a culture that welcomes warnings are critical to effective crisis leadership. But these remain theoretical unless leaders commit to two fundamental disciplines that most organizations discuss but few practice rigorously. The first is genuinely thinking about the downside, not as a pessimistic exercise but as a deliberate planning tool. The second is doing the homework before the crisis arrives, when there's still time to prepare rather than merely react.

These aren't glamorous activities. They don't generate exciting headlines or impressive quarterly results. But when the pressure mounts and decisions need to be made in minutes rather than months, the leaders who survive are the ones who did the unglamorous work beforehand. Let us examine what that actually means in practice.

Organizations expend considerable energy pursuing the upside: growth, visibility, innovation, speed. In most planning sessions, the upside is always talked about. How much money we are going to make, how successful the new project is going to be, basically, it's how wonderful everything is going to end up. Far less time is spent on honestly evaluating the downside. Consequences. Second-order effects. What happens if this fails? What happens if we are wrong? In intelligence, we were trained to live on the downside. Not because we were pessimistic, but because ignoring the downside is how people get hurt. Leaders who plan only for success are gambling with others' lives, careers, and trust.

Think About the Downside

Let's start by considering the downside, which may seem simple but runs counter to how most organizations operate. Leadership meetings naturally gravitate toward optimism and opportunity. Everyone wants to talk about growth projections, market expansion, and competitive advantages. There's social pressure to be the person who sees possibilities rather than problems. Raising potential downsides can make you seem negative, risk-averse, or lacking in vision. But this optimism bias is precisely what gets organizations into trouble. The downside doesn't go away just because nobody wants to discuss it at the planning meeting. It waits patiently until circumstances bring it roaring into view, usually at the worst possible moment.

Thinking about the downside isn't about being pessimistic or killing momentum. It's about stress-testing your plans against reality before reality does the stress-testing for you. What happens if your key assumption proves wrong? What if your main competitor responds differently than you expect? What if the regulatory environment shifts? What if your timeline slips by three months? These aren't comfortable questions, but they're necessary ones. Leaders who ask them early can build contingencies, create backup plans, and position their organizations to pivot when circumstances change. Leaders who avoid them end up making desperate decisions under pressure with no good options available.

The military calls this "red teaming," in which one group deliberately seeks to identify weaknesses in another group's plan. Intelligence agencies call it "analysis of competing hypotheses," where you formally test your assumptions against alternative explanations. Businesses often call it nothing at all, because they skip this step entirely. But whatever you call it, the principle remains the same: your plan needs an adversary before it meets real adversaries. That adversary should be your own team, working through scenarios where things go wrong, not to be defeatist but to be prepared.

Understanding Second-Order Effects

This gap in thinking becomes most dangerous during a crisis, when the pressure to act quickly can blind leaders to the very consequences they need to anticipate most carefully. In the chaos of an emergency, with stakeholders demanding immediate solutions and every minute feeling critical, the natural human response is to grab the nearest tool and start swinging. But in crises, second-order thinking matters most. The decisions made under pressure don't just solve problems; they set in motion chains of events that will shape the organization long after the immediate fire is extinguished. History is littered with examples of crisis responses that seemed brilliant in the moment but created disasters in the long run. The Cobra Effect, a cautionary tale from colonial India, illustrates what happens when leaders focus solely on immediate results without considering how their solutions might backfire. Understanding how actions cascade through complex systems isn't pessimism, it's survival.

When leaders make decisions during a crisis, they naturally focus on solving the immediate problem. But every action creates ripples that extend far beyond the initial solution. These ripples are called second-order effects, and understanding them separates reactive leadership from truly strategic crisis management. A leader might implement a quick fix that addresses today's emergency, only to discover weeks or months later that their solution has created entirely new problems, sometimes worse than the original crisis. The best leaders in high-pressure situations train themselves to think several steps ahead, asking not just "Will this work?" but "What happens next, and what happens after that?"

Consider how a company facing financial trouble might announce immediate layoffs to cut costs. The first-order effect is apparent: expenses drop, and the balance sheet improves. But the second-order effects ripple outward in ways that might not be immediately visible. Remaining employees become anxious and distracted; productivity declines; the best talent quietly begins to seek other positions; and institutional knowledge erodes. Customer service might suffer as understaffed teams struggle to keep up. The company saved money in the short term but may have mortgaged its future recovery. A leader aware of these cascading consequences might choose a different path entirely, perhaps implementing temporary across-the-board pay cuts or identifying creative cost-saving measures that preserve the team's ability to execute when conditions improve.

The Cobra Effect illustrates second-order thinking gone awry.

During British colonial rule in India, officials were concerned about the number of venomous cobras in Delhi. Their solution seemed straightforward: they offered a bounty for every dead cobra brought in. Initially, the program appeared successful, as participants submitted dead snakes and collected their rewards. But then the second-order effects emerged. Enterprising citizens realized they could make easy money by breeding cobras specifically to kill them for the bounty. When the government discovered this scheme and cancelled the program in frustration, the cobra breeders released their now-worthless snakes into the city. The result? Delhi ended up with far more cobras than before the program started. The original problem was compounded by leaders' failure to anticipate how people would respond to their incentives.

The Cobra Effect has become shorthand for well-intentioned policies that backfire spectacularly due to unintended consequences. It reminds us that people are creative and will respond to incentives in ways that leaders might not anticipate. During any crisis, leaders must think like chess players, anticipating how different groups will react to their moves. Will this policy create perverse incentives? Could people game this system? What might people do that we're not expecting? The most effective crisis leaders gather diverse perspectives, stress-test their decisions against different scenarios, and remain humble about their ability to predict every outcome. They build monitoring systems to catch unintended consequences early, and they're willing to pivot quickly when their solutions start creating new problems. In the fog of crisis, this kind of disciplined, multi-layered thinking is what separates leaders who merely survive from those who emerge stronger.

Provide the warning even when nothing happens

One of the toughest parts of any career is speaking up about potential problems, especially when nothing bad ends up happening. It creates an odd professional catch-22. When your warning helps prevent a crisis, it appears you were worried for nothing. The disaster you predicted did not occur, so, in retrospect, your alarm seems unnecessary or even overblown. Over time, people learn a hard lesson: staying quiet feels a lot safer than being labeled the person who always predicts doom. Speaking up can cost you social capital and professional credibility, while keeping your concerns to yourself rarely brings immediate consequences.

But that organizational silence is dangerous. Just because nothing bad happened doesn't mean the warning was wrong. Often, this indicates that the warning was effective. Someone took it seriously, made adjustments, and avoided the crisis. Here's the problem: you can never really prove a negative. You'll never know for sure whether your careful planning prevented disaster or whether it was just your day for trouble. Leaders who repeatedly brush off safety measures and contingency planning because "nothing has happened before" are creating a risk that no insurance policy can cover.

When a leader's ego gets involved, things get even worse. They feel like heroes for making bold decisions that didn't backfire. Then they often punish or dismiss the people who raised concerns, since the disasters were avoided anyway. This teaches exactly the wrong lesson. Instead of encouraging the organization to loudly and proudly prevent failures, it trains everyone to let failures happen quietly and hope for the best.

I've seen organizations inadvertently teach their teams to stop reporting problems, and it happens slowly. An analyst spots an emerging risk and raises a flag. Leadership waves it off. Nothing terrible happens right away. That analyst gets a reputation for "cries wolf" or "doesn't understand the business." Other analysts watch this play out and take notes. They adjust their behavior to match what gets rewarded.

After a few rounds of this, the organization has effectively dismantled its own early warning system. Then, when a real crisis hits, leadership is shocked that no one saw it coming. But here's the truth: people did see it coming. They just learned it wasn't worth mentioning. The warning signs were there, flashing brightly, but everyone had been trained to look away.

The best leaders actively work against this dynamic. They thank people for raising concerns regardless of whether anything bad actually happens. They openly acknowledge that you can't prove what disasters you prevented, only what disasters occurred. They create an environment in which people can voice concerns without encountering defensiveness, eye rolls, or later quiet retaliation. These leaders understand that a culture of speaking up isn't just nice to have, it's the organization's immune system, and it needs constant care to stay healthy.

But even in the healthiest organizations with the most receptive leaders, there's a delicate balance that professionals must navigate. Speaking up is essential, but so is understanding your role within the hierarchy and respecting leadership's ultimate authority to make decisions. This isn't about blind obedience or corporate politics. It's about the practical reality that organizations require clear lines of accountability, and leaders need the authority to make final decisions even when their teams disagree.

The tension here is real and unavoidable. You have a professional obligation to raise concerns, present evidence, and make your case clearly. But you also have a responsibility to recognize when you've done your job, and it's time to let leadership lead. Pushing too hard or too long can undermine trust and damage your credibility for future warnings that might be even more critical. Yet staying silent when you see genuine danger isn't loyalty, it's abdication. Finding the right line between these extremes is one of the hardest judgment calls any professional makes, and no formula works in every situation. It requires reading the room, understanding your leader's decision-making style, and knowing when your voice adds value rather than creates noise.

Do not outthink the boss, but do not be silent either. Every organization has a hierarchy. Pretending otherwise is dishonest. Undermining leadership erodes trust. But silence in the face of known risk is not loyalty. It is avoidance. The responsibility of professionals is to inform leadership clearly, respectfully, and persistently. If leadership chooses not to act, that is their decision. But they should never be able to say they were not warned.

This balance is difficult. It requires judgment. It requires timing. It requires understanding when to push, when to document, and when to step back. But it is essential. Much of what keeps systems functioning is invisible because the best work prevents headlines. The public never sees the near misses. They only see failures. That creates a distorted view of how safety is maintained.

Do the Homework

Now let's talk about doing the homework, which sounds almost offensively basic yet gets violated with astonishing frequency at senior levels. Decisions made without proper context, historical understanding, or knowledge of prior failures aren't bold or innovative. They're negligent. In intelligence operations, homework was survival. Understanding what strategies had been attempted previously, what failed, why they failed, and what lessons were supposedly learned mattered more than any novel idea. The institutional memory of failure is one of the most valuable resources any organization possesses, yet it's routinely ignored in favor of fresh starts and clean slates.

Leaders who shortcut this understanding create systems that appear strong but are fundamentally fragile. They're building on ground they haven't properly surveyed. When stress arrives, these systems fail in predictable ways that proper homework would have revealed. The patterns were there in the historical record, visible to anyone who bothered to look. Still, the leader was too busy being decisive to take the time to learn why previous leaders made different choices.

Doing the homework means reading the post-mortem reports from previous initiatives, especially the failed ones. Most organizations write these reports after significant setbacks, then file them away where they gather digital dust. These documents are gold mines of practical wisdom about what doesn't work in your specific environment with your particular constraints. They represent expensive lessons already paid for. Ignoring them means you're likely to pay for the same lessons all over again, except now on your watch and your budget.

It means talking to people who lived through prior attempts at similar changes. The veterans in your organization carry knowledge that never makes it into official documentation. They remember the informal dynamics, the political landmines, the unexpected obstacles that derailed previous efforts. They know why specific processes exist and what occurs when they are removed. Some of this knowledge might be outdated, but much of it remains relevant. The leader who dismisses these voices as stuck in the past is often the one who repeats the past's mistakes.

It means understanding why specific processes exist before eliminating them as bureaucratic waste. Every established organization has procedures that seem pointless to newcomers. Some of them are indeed pointless, relics of conditions that no longer apply. But many exist because someone learned a hard lesson. That approval process you think is slowing everything down might be preventing the kind of error that cost the company millions five years ago. That redundant check you want to eliminate might be the only thing catching critical mistakes before they reach customers. Before you cut, understand what you're cutting and why it was added in the first place.

It means recognizing that today's "common sense solution" may have been yesterday's failed experiment. Fresh eyes are valuable, and outsiders often spot inefficiencies that insiders have stopped noticing. But there's a reason experienced professionals greet some suggestions with weary recognition rather than enthusiasm. They've seen this movie before. They know how it ends. The proposal that seems innovative and obvious to you may already have been tried three times, each time with modifications, only to create problems that eventually forced a return to the current approach.

It means acknowledging that organizational scar tissue is usually formed for reasons, even if those reasons aren't immediately visible. Companies don't generally create complicated procedures because they enjoy complexity. They make them because something went wrong, and the procedure was meant to prevent it from happening again. Sometimes the cure becomes worse than the disease, and the procedure outlives its usefulness. But sometimes that ugly, awkward process is the only thing standing between normal operations and catastrophic failure. You can't tell the difference without doing the homework.

The most dangerous phrase in organizational life is "we should just..." followed by a suggestion that ignores all contextual complexity. We should combine these departments. We should eliminate this approval step. We should adopt the approach that works at other companies. Seasoned professionals recognize that simplicity is often achieved through ignorance or willful dismissal of complicating factors. Real solutions acknowledge complexity, work within constraints, and respect the hard-won lessons embedded in current systems, even as they push for necessary improvements. That kind of wisdom doesn't come from bold vision. It comes from doing your homework.

Final Reflections

We are safe in spite of ourselves. That sobering truth should echo in the mind of every leader who believes their organization runs smoothly because of perfect planning and flawless execution. We remain safe only because dedicated professionals quietly address gaps, cover weaknesses, and sound alarms that often go unheard. But this fragile safety will hold only if leaders learn to listen sooner, think more carefully about the downside, and create cultures that welcome warnings rather than punish them. The world has grown more complicated and interconnected, with demonstrated hatred and division that can ignite faster than our systems can respond.

The systems we trust are held together by judgment, accommodation, and individual dedication far more than by elegant design or sophisticated technology. Acknowledging this reality isn't defeatist or pessimistic. It's the essential first step toward building genuinely resilient organizations that don't depend on heroic individual effort to compensate for structural inadequacy. The best leaders understand they're managing accommodations, not perfect systems. They know their organizations survive through constant adjustment and human wisdom, not through rigid adherence to documented processes. They create space for judgment rather than demanding blind compliance. They listen to expertise rather than dismissing concern as negativity or fear.

When the expert starts running, these leaders don't ask, "Why are you overreacting?" They ask, "What do you see?" and then they act on the answer. That's the difference between leading through chaos and being consumed by it.

Every major lesson in my career has come down to one truth: chaos doesn't destroy leaders, it reveals them. Whether it was a midnight call from the command post, a client in crisis, or a briefing that went sideways, chaos stripped away whatever I thought I knew and forced me to see clearly. It taught me that leadership isn't about being right, it's about being responsible. The best leaders I've worked with weren't perfect. They made mistakes, sometimes catastrophic ones. But they owned them. They didn't waste energy defending the past; they spent it building the next move. They understood that credibility isn't earned through an unbroken string of success; it's earned through accountability when things fall apart.

Chaos is the purest form of truth. It doesn't care about hierarchy, politics, or credentials. It only responds to competence and composure. When everything falls apart, people follow the one who can still think clearly. That's why leading through chaos isn't about seeking disorder or thriving on crisis; it's about mastering yourself inside it. The STOP technique, upward training, and second-order thinking all point to one fundamental idea: control starts with clarity. If you can control your reactions, you can control the outcome. That's the ultimate leadership paradox: you lead others by first mastering yourself.

We live in a world obsessed with control, metrics, algorithms, strategies, and carefully managed brand narratives. But real leadership doesn't live in control; it lives in response. The world will keep shifting, faster and more unpredictably, every year. The next crisis won't look like the last one. The next generation of leaders won't have the luxury of certainty. They'll need flexibility, empathy, and courage, qualities you can't teach with a PowerPoint slide or capture in a quarterly report.

When I look back at my career, from the streets to the boardrooms, from ghettos to corner offices, I see one constant pattern: the people who lasted, who truly made a difference, were the ones who could pause. They didn't always have the answers, but they knew how to find them without panicking. They understood that the appearance of decisive action matters far less than the quality of the decision itself.

That's what I hope this book gives you. Not a rigid system, not another checklist to follow, but permission to stop. Permission to think when everyone around you is demanding immediate action. Permission to ask hard questions when the room wants easy answers. Because once you stop, you can think. And once you can think, you can lead. The rest, titles, headlines, committees, budgets, and strategic plans, are noise.

Leadership isn't about the system you work in or the sophisticated tools at your disposal. It's about how you behave when those systems fail, and those tools break. It's about the pause before the decision, the calm before the action, the clarity you maintain when chaos surrounds you. That's what leading through chaos means. It's not a slogan or a motivational catchphrase; it's a discipline built through practice, refined through failure, and proven when everything else falls apart.

The next storm is coming. It always is. You won't rise above it by shouting louder or moving faster than everyone else. You won't survive it through perfect planning or superior technology. You'll rise above it by standing still just long enough to see what others can't by thinking about second-order effects, while others chase first-order solutions. By welcoming the warning no one else wants to hear. By doing the homework that everyone else skipped. By acknowledging that we're all safe in spite of ourselves, and that this precarious safety demands constant, humble vigilance.

Then you'll act, with purpose, not panic. With clarity, not chaos. And that's when people will follow. Not because you had all the answers, but because you had the courage to pause, the wisdom to listen, and the composure to lead when it mattered most.

....

That's the leader the world needs now. That leader can be you!

EPILOGUE

If there is one thing I hope you take from this book, it is this: you do not have to hold a title to be a leader. Leadership is not a rank or a position. It is a choice. Anyone can lead. In fact, some of the finest leaders I have encountered in forty years were people who never wore a badge above Detective, never sat in a corner office, and never had their name on a door. They led because they saw what needed to be done and did it. They led because they understood that leadership is about influence, not authority. If you take nothing else from these stories, take that.

Now, as for the state of things, has anything changed since the days I spent navigating turf wars, bureaucratic dysfunction, and organizational paralysis? The answer is yes. And no.

At the government level, particularly regarding our national and municipal response capabilities, things have changed for the better. We are not where we need to be, but we are no longer where we were. After 9/11, after Katrina, after enough catastrophic failures laid bare the cost of institutional ego and information silos, people finally started listening. Emergency management is now treated as a serious discipline. You can earn a master's degree in crisis and consequence management. Universities teach what we used to learn through trial and error and by body count. That is progress.

More importantly, communication between agencies has improved dramatically in some cases. The FBI, which once operated as though local law enforcement existed only to stay out of its way, now maintains a far more open dialogue with municipal and state agencies. Joint task forces, intelligence-sharing protocols, and collaborative operations are no longer the exception. They are the expectation. It took decades, and it took disasters that should never have happened, but the walls finally started coming down. Not all of them. Not everywhere. But enough to matter.

And yet.

For all the structural improvements, for all the frameworks, memoranda of understanding, and interagency partnerships, we still face the same fundamental problem I encountered on day one as a detective in the South Bronx: people. Stupid people. Incompetent people. Manipulative people. People who lie to themselves about their own limitations. People who mistake volume for insight, activity for progress, and compliance for competence. People who, when the moment demands clarity and courage, deliver only noise and self-preservation.

No amount of institutional reform fixes that. You cannot write a policy that prevents ego. You cannot mandate self-awareness. You cannot train someone out of their need to be right at the expense of being effective. These are human problems, and they will persist as long as humans hold power.

Which brings me to a man named Tony Dumont. He was the kind of person who could sit through a three-hour planning session filled with posturing, territorial maneuvering, and performative incompetence, and say, quietly, the same thing he always said.

It was a way of distilling the absurdity of it all into a single sentence. It was not cynical. It was not hopeless. It was simply... true. And every time I heard it, I was reminded that the work continues not because the system is fixed, or because people have suddenly become wiser, but because there are still enough people willing to see the patterns, call out the dysfunction, and do the work anyway.

So yes. Things have improved. But no. We are not done. We never will be. Because the STOP Technique is not a cure. It is a discipline. It requires vigilance. It requires humility. And it requires the willingness to accept that some problems do not have solutions; they have practices. You practice recognizing the warning signs. You practice interrupting your own worst instincts. You practice leading, even when the people around you would rather perform.

If you are in a position of responsibility, you will encounter moments when the system fails you. When politics override the mission. When the organizational chart becomes a shield instead of a structure. When the people who should know better choose comfort over competence. And in those moments, you will have a choice.

You can be part of the problem. Or you can stop, think, and be part of the solution.

That is the work. That is the challenge. And that is what Tony understood better than most.

"Humanity never fails to disappoint."
—Tony Dumont

THE END

BOOK SAL LIFRIERI TO SPEAK AT YOUR NEXT EVENT

When Chaos Hits, Will Your Leaders Freeze or Lead?

Most leadership training teaches people what to do when everything goes right.

Sal Lifrieri teaches them what to do when everything goes wrong.

With over 40 years on the front lines of crisis, from NYPD Homicide Detective to member of the elite NYPD Hostage Negotiation Team, to Director of Security and Intelligence Operations for New York City's Office of Emergency Management, Sal has seen leadership fail in every way imaginable. He's negotiated with armed suspects, stood in command centers during terrorist threats, and navigated the chaos of 9/11. Now he shares those hard-won lessons with organizations that refuse to sugarcoat the reality of leadership under pressure.

No motivational fluff. No feel-good platitudes. Just brutal honesty about how decisions actually get made when the pressure is on.

SPEAKING TOPICS INCLUDE:

KEYNOTE PRESENTATIONS (60-90 minutes) – Leading Through Chaos: When Systems Fail and Politics Trump Safety – The STOP Technique: Structured Decision-Making Under Pressure – We Are Safe In Spite of Ourselves: The Hidden Failures Behind Every Crisis

WORKSHOPS & TRAINING – Half-day workshops (3-4 hours) – Full-day intensive programs (6-8 hours) – Multi-session leadership development – Custom programs tailored to your organization

PERFECT FOR:

Corporate leadership teams • Security & risk management professionals • Law enforcement & first responders • Government agencies • Healthcare organizations • Emergency management teams • Any organization where decisions carry real consequences

Don't wait for the next crisis to discover your leaders aren't ready.

BOOK SAL LIFRIERI TODAY – CALL (914) 576-8706

contact@sallifrieri.com

www.sallifrieri.com

REFERENCES

Agency for Toxic Substances and Disease Registry. "Part 2: What Are Cholinesterase Inhibitors?" CDC ATSDR Case Studies in Environmental Medicine. Accessed February 7, 2026. https://archive.cdc.gov/#/details?q=gov/csem/cholinesterase-inhibitors/inhibitors.html&start=0&rows=10&url=https://www.atsdr.cdc.gov/csem/cholinesterase-inhibitors/inhibitors.html

Associated Press. "Security Costs Soar for GOP Convention: Just Last Month, the Estimate Was $47 Million to $65 Million." NBC News, May 11, 2004. Accessed February 7, 2026. https://www.nbcnews.com/id/wbna4951785

Best, Richard A., Jr. *Open Source Intelligence (OSINT): Issues for Congress.* CRS Report RL34270. Washington, DC: Congressional Research Service, December 5, 2007. Accessed February 7, 2026.

Brookings Institution. "Housing Families Displaced by Katrina: A Review of the Federal Response to Date." November 1, 2005. Accessed February 7, 2026.

Centers for Disease Control and Prevention. "Strategic National Stockpile (SNS)." CDC Emergency Preparedness and Response. Accessed February 7, 2026.

De Becker, Gavin. The Gift of Fear: Survival Signals That Protect Us from Violence. Boston: Little, Brown and Company, 1997.

Doyle, Charles. "The Posse Comitatus Act and Related Matters: The Use of the Military to Execute Civilian Law." Congressional Research Service. November 6, 2018. Accessed February 7, 2026.

Electronic Code of Federal Regulations. "14 CFR 121.309, Emergency Equipment." Accessed February 7, 2026. https://www.ecfr.gov/current/title-14/chapter-I/subchapter-G/part-121/subpart-K/section-121.309

Encyclopaedia Britannica. "Mohammed Saeed al Sahhaf." *Encyclopaedia Britannica*. Accessed February 7, 2026.

Federal Bureau of Investigation. "World Trade Center Bombing 1993." FBI History. Accessed February 7, 2026. https://www.fbi.gov/history/famous-cases/world-trade-center-bombing-1993

Federal Emergency Management Agency. "Urban Search and Rescue." FEMA. July 29, 2025. Accessed February 7, 2026. https://www.fema.gov/emergency-managers/national-preparedness/frameworks/urban-search-rescue

Friedman, Robert I. "Brighton Beach Goodfellas." Vanity Fair, January 1993. Accessed February 7, 2026. https://vanityfair.azurewebsites.net/article/1993/1/brighton-beach-goodfellas

Heisler, Elayne J. "The Strategic National Stockpile: Overview and Issues for Congress." Congressional Research Service. September 26, 2023. Accessed February 7, 2026.

Kerr, James. Legacy: What the All Blacks Can Teach Us About the Business of Life. New York: Little, Brown and Company, 2013.

McChrystal, Stanley. "Listen, Learn … Then Lead." TED Talk, February 2011. https://www.ted.com/talks/stanley_mcchrystal_listen_learn_then_lead

Merriam Webster. "Confidential." Merriam Webster.com Dictionary. Accessed February 7, 2026.

Merriam Webster. "Stupid." Merriam Webster.com Dictionary. Accessed February 7, 2026.

National Hurricane Center. "Tropical Cyclone Report: Hurricane Katrina, 23–30 August 2005." National Oceanic and Atmospheric Administration. PDF. Accessed February 7, 2026.

National Hurricane Center. Hurricane Hortense, 3 to 16 September 1996. Tropical Cyclone Report. National Oceanic and Atmospheric Administration, October 23, 1996. PDF. Accessed February 7, 2026. https://www.nhc.noaa.gov/data/tcr/AL081996_Hortense.pdf

National Transportation Safety Board. In flight Breakup Over the Atlantic Ocean, Trans World Airlines Flight 800, Boeing 747 131, N93119, Near East Moriches, New York, July 17, 1996. Aircraft Accident Report NTSB AAR 00 03. Washington, DC, National Transportation Safety Board, 2000. PDF. Accessed February 7, 2026. https://www.ntsb.gov/investigations/accidentreports/reports/aar0003.pdf

Office of the Director of National Intelligence. "Annex 3: The Central Intelligence Agency's CIA Report." Intelligence Community, "IC on the Record" Declassified Database. Accessed February 7, 2026.

Office of the Mayor of the City of New York. "Mayor Giuliani, Speaker Vallone Report on Status of Relief Effort in Puerto Rico; Announce Next Steps." Press Release Archives, September 19, 1996. Accessed February 7, 2026. https://www.nyc.gov/html/om/html/96/sp448-96.html

Pfeffer, Jeffrey. *Leadership BS: Fixing Workplaces and Careers One Truth at a Time*. New York: HarperBusiness, 2015.

Powell, Colin L. *My American Journey*. New York: Random House, 1995.

Sinek, Simon. Leaders Eat Last: Why Some Teams Pull Together and Others Don't. New York: Portfolio/Penguin, 2014.

Sugiyama, Akihiro, et al. "The Tokyo Subway Sarin Attack Has Long Term Effects on Survivors: A 25 Year Follow Up Study." Occupational and Environmental Medicine (2020). Accessed February 7, 2026.

The White House. "Homeland Security Presidential Directive 3." March 12, 2002. Accessed February 7, 2026. https://georgewbush-whitehouse.archives.gov/news/releases/2002/03/20020312-5.html

Transportation Security Administration. "Security Screening." TSA. Accessed February 7, 2026. https://www.tsa.gov/travel/security-screening

Transportation Security Administration. "Snow Globes." What Can I Bring? TSA. April 5, 2017. Accessed February 7, 2026. https://www.tsa.gov/travel/security-screening/whatcanibring/items/snow-globes

U.S. Army Military Intelligence Corps Hall of Fame. "Lieutenant General Samuel V. Wilson." PDF. Accessed February 7, 2026.

U.S. Department of Homeland Security. "Secretary Napolitano Announces Implementation of National Terrorism Advisory System." April 20, 2011. Accessed February 7, 2026. https://www.dhs.gov/archive/news/2011/04/20/secretary-napolitano-announces-implementation-national-terrorism-advisory-system

U.S. Naval War College Library. "Intelligence Studies: Types of Intelligence Collection." LibGuides. Accessed February 7, 2026.

U.S. Transportation Command. "Military Sealift Command Hospital Ship to Support NYC." USTRANSCOM News, 2001. Accessed February 7, 2026. https://www.ustranscom.mil/cmd/panewsreader.cfm?ID=2888C681-5056-A127-59EA3DB243D03367&yr=2001&

United Press International. "UPI Focus: Army Probes Possible Nerve Gas Find." March 27, 1997. Accessed February 7, 2026. https://www.upi.com/Archives/1997/03/27/UPI-Focus-Army-probes-possible-nerve-gas-find/7154859438800/

United States Code. "10 U.S.C. 948a(2), Classified Information." Legal Information Institute, Cornell Law School. Accessed February 7, 2026. https://www.law.cornell.edu/definitions/uscode.php?def_id=10-USC-1336325791-357709045

White, Ron. Ron White: You Can't Fix Stupid. Directed by Michael Drumm. Comedy Central, 2006. Accessed February 7, 2026. https://www.tvguide.com/tvshows/ron-white-you-cant-fix-stupid/cast/1000219434/

www.ingramcontent.com/pod-product-compliance
Lightning Source LLC
Chambersburg PA
CBHW070419290526
45791CB00005B/1749